THE SECRETS OF NUMEROLOGY

The Secrets of Numerology

Numbers and Human Fortune

ATUL SEHGAL

GYAN PUBLISHING HOUSE
New Delhi 110002

The Secrets of Numerology
Numbers and Human Fortune
(Occult Science, General Interest)

ISBN : 81-212-0565-4

Published in 1997 in India by
Gyan Publishing House
5, Ansari Road
New Delhi 110 002

Laser Typeset at Akshar, Delhi
Printed at Mehra Offset Press, New Delhi.

Contents

Preface

We all use numbers in our daily life. From childhood to old age numbers help us in many ways to maintain our records. We cannot imagine the world without numbers. We make thousands of permutations and combinations of the numbers 0 to 9 and their application in all facets and spheres of our life is total. Numbers appear to dictate the affairs of our civilization from micro to macro levels. In fact, so entrenched are numbers in our daily life that our civilized existence seems to be meaningless without them. We get a number tag—the number of the cradle at the maternity centre, the moment we are born! And numbers chase us right till the graveyard or crematorium where graves or cremation beds are identified by numbers. In between birth and death, it is again these numbers which define our homes, dresses, cars, heights, weights and girths, intelligence levels, riches, etc.

You may have sometimes wondered whether numbers were invented by man or they are primordial entities. Perhaps the truth is that numbers are indeed prehistoric, primordial entities, which gives them a mystic, divine dimension. According to Hindu scriptures, the concept of numbers was contained in the divine books called Vedas. Vedas embody the fragments of ultimate knowledge passed on by the Supreme Divinity to mankind. And this philosophy appeals to the rational human mind too. For nature reveals itself beautifully through numbers. We observe wonderful periodicity and repetitiveness in the phenomena of nature which are accurately explained through numbers. Numbers have a remarkable occult significance too. Thus the past, present and future events—all can be described through the working of numbers. Admittedly, numbers are the instruments of God Almighty, who is the Supreme Creator, Controller, Benefactor and Destroyer of the Universe.

Have you ever thought, why there are 7 seas (the Arctic, Antarctic, North Atlantic, South Atlantic, North Pacific, South Pacific and Indian Ocean), 7 notes of music (Sa, Re, Ga, Ma, Pa, Dha, Ni), 7 colours in the rainbow (Violet, Indigo, Blue, Green, Yellow, Orange and Red), 7 days in a week (Sunday, Monday, Tuesday, Wednesday, Thursday, Friday and Saturday), 7 'Rishis' or Sages (Marichi, Atri, Angirasu, Pulastya, Pulah, Kratu and Vashishta), 7 constituent elements of the human body (Chyle, Blood, Flesh, Fat, Bone, Marrow and Semen), 7 constituent parts of a kingdom (King, Ministers, Ally, Territory, Fortress, Army and Treasury), and 7 Puris (*saptapuri*), i.e., seven principal places of Hindu Pilgrimage (Ayodhya, Mathura, Hardwar, Kashi, Kanchi, Ujjain and Dwarka)? Truly, the number 7 must be having some unique significance fixed by God Almighty. The number 7 is the number which represents the mystic, spiritual side of nature. It forms the foundation upon which the edifice of material nature is built.

Consider now the number 4. Those are 4 seasons (Spring, Summer, Rainy and Winter), 4 directions (North, East, West, South), 4 original castes or 'Varnas' in Hindu society (Brahmin, Kshatriya, Vaishya and Shudra), 4 states of matter (Solid, Liquid, Gaseous and the Plasma state) and 4 physical dimensions (comprising the 3 spatial dimensions and time as the fourth dimension). All these observations indicate that nature reveals itself through specific numbers which have special meanings and significance. The number 4 represents the physical side of nature rather than the spiritual.

In a similar way, the significations of all other numbers 0, 1, 2, 3, 5, 6, 8 and 9 can be discovered and one has only to marvel at the role played by numbers in man's co-existence and interaction with mother nature.

This little book is not intended to be a mere teaching material on Numerology but much more than that it is aimed at the common man as an interesting, educative reading material and an effective aid to use the science of numbers for his better living. Numerology can, indeed, be used as a practical tool for man to understand his own self better, to discover his innate strengths, to uncover his weaknesses, to harmonise his association with his surroundings, to make optimum utilisation of his resources and opportunities and to avert or mitigate adversities in his life. True, to a great extent, man is tied to his destiny. But knowledge gives us power to stand adversity even if it must befall us and in many cases knowledge provides a forewarning of impending dangers. And knowledge enlightens us on the best use of opportunities that come our way.

How numbers work for you, work behind you and work against you is revealed in the following pages. The various chapters attempt to take a refreshingly practical look at the occult significations of numbers. Above all, endeavour all through has been to highlight the practical utility of this knowledge in the daily life of human mortals.

9.7.1997 **ATUL SEHGAL**

CHAPTER 1

Numbers: Basic Characteristics and Significations

Each number possesses specific characteristics. These characteristics, seen along with the various physical and mundane significations, render each number an important entity. And the importance of each number really stems from its esoteric relationship with planets and zodiac signs which control all mundane phenomena as per classical Astrology.

Let us begin with zero, represented as the numeral 0. In the opinion of many scholars of Numerology, the zero is not a pure number. It has its own significance in as much as it represents universe—the divine whole. It stands for divine continuum or eternity. This is borne out by the results of the operation of zero on other numerals.

$$0 \times 1 = 0$$
$$0 \times 2 = 0$$
$$0 \times 5 = 0$$
$$0 \times 9 = 0$$

The above multiplicative operations indicate that zero stands for the universe and all other numerals, whatever they may represent, cannot alter the character of zero through interaction.

The number 1 represents creation in its prime form. It stands for independence and fundamental creative energy. This number symbolises the Sun, which is the largest celestial body in our planetary system. Below are indicated the characteristics and significations of this number.

Characteristics: Large, masculine, fiery, hot, orange coloured, authoritative, powerful, affable, charitable, generous, dignified, arrogant, pompous, independent, assertive, etc.

Significations: Eastern direction, soul, temperament, health, kingdom, father, eyes, heart, bile, digestion, pride, ego, hobbies, respect, government, royal authority, power, prestige, exuberance, executive, manager, medicine, physician, gold, etc.

Thus anything that is large or fiery or powerful, etc., has the influence of number 1 behind it. Similarly, this number signifies soul, eastern terrestrial direction, kingdom, etc.

The number 2 also represents creation but in a secondary or derived form. It symbolises the moon and partakes its natural characteristics. Let us cite its major characteristics and significations.

Characteristics: Feminine, cold, watery, white, fair complexioned, sensitive, changeable, soft, delicate, polite, timid, etc.

Significations: Western direction, mind and mental phenomena, affluence, mother, home and residence, phlegm, lymph, milk, breasts, silver, public, domestic affairs, sensationalism, etc.

This number is the signifactor of mind and is, therefore, considered very important. The human mind is the seat of all emotions —anger, hatred, love, joy, happiness, sadness, excitement, fear, frustration, jealousy, jubilation, etc. The urge, motivation to perform various deeds—good or bad really takes root in the mind. As such the mind is attached such prime importance in human existence. The number 2 represents mind and various emotional factors that engender desire and drive to perform mundane tasks.

The number 3 stands for Jupiter, the largest among planets revolving around the Sun. It symbolises pride, ambition and prudence. It represents divine knowledge and its application in the material world. For this number, note the following.

Characteristics: Temperate, hot, masculine, sanguine, composed, prudent, ambitious, fortunate, yellow coloured, progressive, etc.

Significations: North-eastern direction, growth, expansion, religion, teachers, priests, offspring, wealth, fat, liver, law, justice, banking, treasure, counsellors and advisors, consultants, management, etc.

Number 3 is a powerful materialistic number that impels growth, expansion and rise. It stands in relationship to divine knowledge that enlightens us in our material pursuits as well as shows us the path leading to salvation. Salvation is the state of ultimate bliss of the human soul when it is freed from the bondage of birth and deaths.

This takes us to the number 4. Number 4 is a strange, weird number though powerful in the material sense. It is, however, laden with contradictions which provide the element of strangeness. Let us first have a look at its basic characteristics and significations.

Characteristics: Extremely intelligent or a near idiot, extremely strong or extremely weak, extremely tall or extremely short.....this number characterizes extremes of all human qualities. Other significations are—greedy, avaricious, opulent, corrupt, unique and conspicuous by virtue of any special feature, deceptive, unconventional, etc.

Significations: Duality, misunderstanding, impurity, misrepresentation, corruption, scams and scandals, illegitimate wealth, research, inventions, computers, space technology, electricity, electronics, etc.

The number 4 stands in symbolism for the planet 'Rahu', a shadowy planet of which we find detailed exposition in classical Hindu Astrology. It may be mentioned in this connection that Hindu Astrology does not recognize in its analytical text the existence of trans-saturnine planets, viz., Uranus, Neptune and Pluto. Rather it does not take cognizance of these planets as exercising separate, individual influence on the earth and its natives. This is not to say that these planets do not exist at all. The fact is that in so far as their astrological influences on the earth and its natives are concerned, these planets are not considered in Hindu Astrology. Whatever influences emanate from them are accounted for in the influences ascribed to two shadowy planets called 'Rahu' and 'Ketu'. The number 4 stands for the planet 'Rahu'.

In Western astrology, however, the number 4 represents Uranus and assumes various characteristics and attributes of this planet. Some of the notable characteristics are—Eccentricity, mysterious, changeable, odd, unique, unconventional, extremist and different.

This takes us to the number 5. This number represents the planet Mercury. Mercury is the smallest planet in the solar system. Below are mentioned the prominent significations and characteristics of the number 5.

Characteristics: Changeable, sensitive, flexible, green coloured, indecisive, witty, humourous, crisp and quick, etc.

Significations: Speech, communication, writing, journalism, education and educational aids, business, trade, stocks and shares, etc.

The number 5 is characterised by some very special qualities—flexibility, adjustability and adaptability. It is highly impressionable and sensitive to surrounding influences.

The number 6 represents Venus, the planet of love, arts, pleasure and beauty. Let us see briefly its characteristics and significations.

Characteristics: Effeminate, amorous, affectionate, sexy, beautiful, pleasurable, artistic, appealing, white coloured, etc.

Significations: Elegance, sex organs, music, songs, plays, comforts, easy-going, jewels, gems, ornaments, conveyances, aristocrats, poets, courtship, marriage, entertainment, decoration, socialising, gambling, casinos, holidays, etc.

This number represents the baser aspects of human life in the material sphere. It stands for everything connected with enjoyment of the senses. It is not a creative number; rather it symbolises all that pertains to spending and consumption of pleasurable material objects.

Next we come over to the number 7. This number stands in symbolism to the planet Neptune as per Western Astrology. However, as per the classical Hindu Astrology, this number symbolises the shadowy planet 'Ketu'. It is a mystic number and signifies the spiritual force behind all worldly creation and phenomena. The important characteristics and significations of this number are represented below.

Characteristics: Lucky and fortunate, tricky, intrinsically strong and powerful, religious, explosive, aggressive, licentious, etc.

Significations: Spiritual experiences and phenomena, marine travel, dreams, clairvoyance, intuition, premonition, mysticism, witchcraft, telepathy, etc.

The number 7 denotes the working of the spiritual side of nature. A brief exposition of the expressions of this number has already been given. To reiterate the same, the number 7 expresses itself through seven heavens, seven seas, seven fundamental notes of music, etc.—which indicates that this number mirrors the spiritual side of nature, the spiritual working behind all the material and worldly activities.

The number 8 stands for the planet Saturn. It is a fatalistic number and represents the working of divine retribution on the earthly plane. Let us see what are the main characteristics and significations of this number.

Characteristics: Rigid, stubborn, hard taskmaster, black coloured, silent, intolerant, miserly, timid, restrictive, unfortunate, etc.

Significations: Low-caste and low-status people, adversities in general, retardation and retrogression, iron, coal, mining and miners, misfortunes, magic, astrology, mathematics, etc.

The number 8 is often associated with calamities and misfortunes. But this is only a superficial truth. The underlying hidden fact is that it stands for divine retribution—which is the working of nature to reward us for our good deeds and punish us for our misdeeds.

The last number in the fundamental series of numbers is 9. This is also a materialistic number and stands for the material and physical energy, force and dynamic activity. It stands in symbolism for the planet Mars. The characteristics and significations of this number are given hereunder.

Characteristics: Energetic, red coloured, strong, brave, violent, destructive, impulsive, fast, inflammatory, expansive, etc.

Significations: Blood, wars, conflicts, volcanic eruptions, earthquakes, fires, landed property, siblings, weapons, etc.

This number is considered a fortunate number by occult scientists provided the violent and impulsive nature associated with it is suitably controlled and channelised.

CHAPTER 2

Simple and Compound Numbers

The numbers 1, 2, 3, 4, 5, 6, 7, 8 and 9 are the simple numbers which form the entire edifice of material entities and things. They also represent spiritual forces and phenomena working behind material activities. This chapter is devoted to the correspondence between simple numbers and terrestrial entities. It also renders a very brief account of compound numbers, i.e., numbers extending from 10 to 52. Numbers beyond 52 are only repetitions of lower numbers, since the basic vibration of numbers remains identical through the series formed by successively adding 9 to the original compound numbers. The numbers 1, 2, 3....up to 9 represent fundamental mundane entities as explained below.

Numbers and days of the week: Appreciate the one-to-one correspondence between the following numbers and days of the week.

Numbers	*Days of week*
1	Sunday (Midnight to Midday)
2	Monday (Midnight to Midday)
3	Thursday
4	Sunday (Midday to Midnight)
5	Wednesday
6	Friday
7	Monday (Midday to Midnight)
8	Saturday
9	Tuesday

It is interesting to observe here that 1 and 4 both represent

Sunday, the former stands for first half of Sunday and the latter for second half. Similarly, 2 and 7 stand for Monday for the first half and second half respectively. Again, it would not be out of place to mention here that Western numerology assigns to the number 4, the planet Uranus and to 7 the planet Neptune. Uranus is considered to be related to Sun and Neptune to Moon. That explains the correspondence.

Numbers and months of the year: Before going over to the relationship between numbers and months of the year, it would be proper to throw light on the zodiac divisions, signs and their correspondence with various months of the calendar year. We know that the entire zodiac comprises twelve parts of astrological significance. Zodiac, as is well known, is the giant circular strip containing planets, stars and other celestial bodies. The zodiac is divided into twelve equal parts called divisions of the zodiac. Each zodiac division is marked by specific characteristics and influences the earth and earthlings in its own special way. Zodiac divisions are also called signs of the zodiac. According to Hindu Astrology the twelve zodiac signs correspond to months of the calendar year as represented below.

The first sign of the zodiac is Aries which extends from 13th April to 12th May. In fact, going by the Hindu Astrology, this period corresponds to the period of transit of Sun through the first house of the zodiac. Mars is the ruler of this sign and the ruling number of the sign is 9.

The second sign of the zodiac is Taurus that begins on 13th May and ends on 14th June. This sign has been assigned the number 6 as the ruling planet of the sign is Venus.

The third sign of the zodiac is Gemini extending from 15th June to 15th July. This Mercurial sign has been assigned the number 5.

The fourth sign of the zodiac called Cancer begins on 16th July and extends till 16th August. This watery sign is ruled by the moon and represented by the number 2.

Leo, the fifth zodiac sign extending from 17th August to 16th September, is represented by the number 1 symbolic of Sun, the largest celestial body of our planetary system.

Then, we come over to Virgo, the sixth sign of the zodiac. This practical, earthy sign is again ruled by Mercury and the number that represents this sign is 5. The period of Virgo begins from 17th September and extends till 16th October.

Next in the zodiac comes Libra, the airy signal ruled by the magnetic planet Venus. Number 6 rules this sign. This sign covers the period from 17th October till 13th November.

The next sign of the zodiac is Scorpio whose period begins on 14th November and extends till 14th December. This sign of the zodiac is ruled by the planet Mars and the number 9.

Sagittarius covering the period from 15th December to 13th January is the sign that follows Scorpio. Sagittarius is ruled by Jupiter and the corresponding ruling number is 3.

After Sagittarius, we come over to Capricorn. This sign covers the period 14th January to 13th February. Capricorn is ruled by Saturn which is represented by the number 8.

The next sign in the zodiac, Aquarius is also ruled by Saturn and is, therefore, assigned the number 8. This sign has the period extending from 14th February to 13th March.

The last sign in the zodiac is Pisces which covers the period extending from 14th March to 12th April. This sign is ruled by Jupiter. Naturally, therefore, the corresponding ruling number is 3.

It must be mentioned in this connection that if we are to assign numbers to complete months of the year viz. January, February, March etc., we would assign the numbers 1, 2, 3, 4, etc., to January, February, March, April, etc. respectively in keeping with the sequence of these months as commonly known and followed.

The correspondence between single numbers 1 to 9 and days of the week as well as months of the year was necessary to establish direct relationship between numbers and the ruling planets. Since all mundane activities are directly influenced and governed by the nine planets including the Sun and the Moon, simple numbers in their own right assume fundamental significance.

In classical Astrology, the entire human population inhabiting the earth is divisible into twelve birth signs corresponding to the above periods of the zodiac. Each period of the zodiac has its own characteristics which are naturally imbibed by the natives of the period. A person born in the zodiac sign of Virgo is fastidious, critical and puritanical. Now when we have assigned a specific number to Virgo, that number 5 assumes all the characteristics of Virgo. Numbers, therefore, are elementary Astrological entities.

Compound Numbers: Having rendered an account of the simple numbers, an exposition of compound numbers becomes necessary. When we count from 9 upwards, we obtain 10, 11, 12, 13, etc. in the endless series of natural numbers. All these numbers from 10 onwards are called compound numbers. Interestingly, each compound number has a distinct identity of its own. However, this distinct identity and character is possessed only by numbers up to 52. Beyond 52, all the natural numbers are reducible to smaller compound numbers less than 52 and have the same characteristics. Hence although each compound number is said to have distinct character and identity, the essential compound numbers comprise those numbers that lie between 10 and 52 with the terminal numbers 10 and 52 included. This would be well illustrated by the following example.

Number 53 has the same characteristics as 44.

Number 56 has the same meaning as 47.

Number 75 has the same character as 48..... and so on.

Compound numbers are obtained by summing up the simple numbers as, when and where they arise. For example, consider a most common mundane event—the birth of a person. Let us say, that person was born on 24th November, 1963. Now that person is characterised by the following simple numbers.

24 — birthdate number

11 — Number of the month November

19 — Compound number formed by adding up the individual numbers 1, 9, 6 and 3.

Having obtained the compound numbers 24, 11 and 19 we observe that the same can be further reduced into simple numbers as follows.

24 into 2 + 4 = 6

11 into 1 + 1 = 2

and 19 into 1 + 9 = 10 = 1 + 0 = 1

Thus, finally we arrive at the numbers 6, 2 and 1 which when summed up yield the number 9. It is a co-incidence that the final number obtained in this case turns out to be a simple number. Consider now another birthdate—8th September 1957. In this case, the respective numbers are as given below.

8 - birthdate number
9 - birth month number
1957
= 22 - birth year number
= 2 + 2
= 4

Thus the three numbers that result are 8, 9 and 4 which when added together give a compound number of 21.

Correspondence of simple numbers with colours: Various simple numbers are characteristic of different colours and this correspondence is represented below.

Number	*Colour*
1	Orange
2	Off white with bluish tinge
3	Yellow
4	Mixed colour/Variegated hues
5	Green
6	White
7	Blue
8	Black
9	Red

It is clear from the above that all white objects are governed by the number 6 and all red things by the number 9. However, for human beings, specific colours or colour combinations are considered lucky for various individuals. A detailed account of this would be rendered later in this book.

Simple numbers and lucky stones or gems: As mentioned above, certain specific colours are deemed to be lucky for various persons. This is because the natural vibrations of that colour match the natural vibrations of birth number of the person. In a similar way, lucky stones or gems also have their own numbers. If the number of a gem is compatible with the birth number of a person, that gem is considered lucky for the person. The following table gives the names of various gems and the birth numbers compatible with those gems.

Birth number	*Gem*
1	Ruby
2	Pearl
3	Topaz
4	Hassonite
5	Emerald
6	Diamond
7	Cat's Eye
8	Sapphire
9	Coral

Both Simple and compound numbers have their own importance in astrological analyses of the past, present and future of human individuals. Simple numbers are fundamental entities, compound numbers are derived entities. But the remarkable fact about Numerology is that the entire vast subject of occultism can be described, studied, analysed and applied through primary natural numbers. As if the Lord Creator first conceived numbers and then set about the task of building the entire universe!

Simple numbers and names: Numerology has assigned simple numbers to various alphabets of English. By summing up the numbers corresponding to each alphabet constituting a name, we obtain the compound number corresponding to that name. This compound number can, thereafter, be reduced into a simple number. The various alphabets are awarded numbers as given below.

A	1	B	2
C	3	D	4
E	5	F	8
G	3	H	5
I	1	J	1

K	2	L	3
M	4	N	5
O	7	P	8
Q	1	R	2
S	3	T	4
U	6	V	6
W	6	X	5
Y	1	Z	7

Let us consider a person named RAM PRAKASH and assign the numbers to various alphabets making his name.

R	A	M	P	R	A	K	A	S	H
2	1	4	8	2	1	2	1	3	5
	7					22 or 4			

Now 7+4 yields 11 or 2. Thus Ram Prakash is characterised by the simple number 2.

CHAPTER 3

Numbers and Human Natives

While discussing about simple and compound numbers and their characteristics and significations in the context of human natives, doubts may have crept in the minds of readers about the specific application of numbers in the astrological analysis of human natives' lives. There is a number representing the birth date of a person— which is called the birth number. In a similar way numbers denote the birth month, the zodiac sign and also the year of birth. As if this is not enough, there is another relevant number—the number of the weekday on which the person was born. We are thus faced with a multiplicity of numbers representing essentially the same event, i.e., birth of the person. Which number is to be applied, in which context and how it is to be applied in astrological analysis of the person's life are the pertinent questions which should be answered. This chapter answers these questions and describes the significance of each number governing the native's birth event directly or indirectly.

Birth number: If a person is born on the 3rd of any month, his birth number is 3. This number has great influence in shaping his individual life. For a person born on 13-8-1944, this number would be 4.

Universality number: Universality number is another name given to the birth-month number. This number has the say in influencing the routine affairs of the native. Let us presume that a person was born on 13th August 1944. His month of birth is August which has the number 8. Therefore, universality number of the person is 8. This number will shape up minor, routine events and activities in the native's life.

Fortune number: This number has control over the current or ongoing period of a person's life and influences all the events during that period. The fortune number is the simple number derived from the number of the birth year. Thus, taking the above example, the birth year of the person is 1944 whose digits add up to 18 and this yields a simple number of 9.

Complete number: This number controls the complete event in a persons past, present, as well as future. This number is arrived at by adding up the Birth number, Universality number and the Fortune number. In the example cited, the complete number works out as follows.

Complete number = Birth number + Universality number + Fortune number.
= 4 + 8 + 9
= 21 = 2 + 1 = 3.

Ascendant number: This number governs the mental traits and character of the person. The ascendant number is the number corresponding to the period of the zodiac sign of the birth. While giving the brief account of various zodiac signs, their periods and the governing numbers in Chapter 2, the ascendant numbers, therefore, have already been given. Taking the previous example of the date of birth as 13-8-1944, the ascendant number is 2 as it corresponds to the zodiac sign of cancer.

Life number: Life number has the profoundest and most wide ranging influence on a person. Life number is that which repeats itself most among the various numbers determined above, viz., Birth number, Universality number, Fortune number, Complete number and the Ascendant number. In case, however, no number repeats itself even once, the Birth number is deemed to be the Life number and shall have the maximum control over life affairs of the person. To sum up the above statements, the life number is the most important number influencing the life affairs of a human native. Next in importance and influence are the birth number, the ascendant number— the universality number, the fortune number and the complete number in order.

Let us once again illustrate the determination of all these numbers for a different birth date say 12th February 1973.

Here Birth number	=	3 (derived from 12)
Universality number	=	2
Fortune number	=	2 (derived from 1973)
Complete number	=	7 (3+2+2)
Ascendant number	=	8 (for Capricorn)

From the above we observe that number 2, repeats itself where none other number does. We, therefore, take 2 as the life number.

In the absence of the life number it is the birth number which is considered to possess the greatest hold over a person in his journey through life.

CHAPTER 4

An Exposition of the Numbers 1 to 9

The number 1: The number 1 is the primary number of all creation. It symbolises Sun, the largest celestial body of the solar system.

If you have number 1 as your life number then you are independent, egoistic, generous, magnanimous and exuberant. You are rigid in your ideas and convictions. You also possess a high degree of self-confidence. However, in many cases an excess of self-assurance can lead to over-confidence which is liable to impair your judgement. Similarly, an excess of self-esteem can result in egotism which again is detrimental to your interest. Nevertheless, you are a prominent, majestic presence in any gathering or group and your regality of attitudes and actions creates wonderful impact on people around you.

All said and done, you are a royal, majestic personality and, perhaps, a born leader. The instinct of leadership comes naturally to you. However, your personality type is not without its negative traits. You are often so outspoken that in a bid to put forth your honest opinion or plain facts known to you, you hurt the sentiments of others and often create bitter enemies. If only people were as broad-minded and forthright as you are, you would never embitter anyone. But human mortals have shortcomings. And common people can hardly digest bitter truth and irritating facts. Perhaps such facts and truth could be better passed on in a diplomatic manner, by sugar coating them. Another negative characteristic of your personality is a tendency to force your opinion on others. This also sometimes results in straining of relationships with other people. An honest advice for you is to be more accommodating in your discussions with others and try not to yield to feelings that tend to nurse your ego. Ego indeed undermines your judgement power. That is an area where you need to be careful.

Which takes us back to your positive attributes. You are hard working and many among you are nearly indefatigable with a lot of stamina and endurance. You are progressive by nature and seek power, authority and prosperity. You are also optimistic and often try to fight your way out of troubles with a never-say-die attitude. And your zest and enthusiasm is infectious. You are also bold in taking decisions and implementing them.

It is said that excess of everything is bad. Your negative attributes really stem from this adage. You tend to indulge in profligacy of spending in order to keep up your royal image. And this works to your disadvantage. You also find it difficult to keep secrets in your mind. Perhaps that is the price of being too open minded. More often than not, you are also suspicious and skeptic. You are advised to avoid being dictatorial in your behaviour. Human bonds are built on reciprocal behaviour. So remember—trying to be forceful and dictatorial can either make people sulk at you or retort in a similar dictatorial way.

Lucky days and years: 1st, 10th, 19th, 28th, 37th, 46th, 55th, 64th, 73rd and 92nd years of your life are significant from the point of view of important events, changes, etc.

Sunday, Monday, Tuesday and Thursday are your lucky days out of which Sunday is your luckiest day.

Your lucky numbers are all that add up to 1.

Complementary numbers: Numbers 2, 3 and 9 are complementary to your life number and hence are also your lucky numbers. You can safely select a person of life number 1, 2, 3 or 9 as your life partner and are also advised to spend a little extra to take a car with number adding upto 1, 2, 3 or 9 when going for its delivery.

The brilliant, attractive personality of number 1 persons attracts members of the opposite sex to them. But number 1 persons expect too much in love and sometimes when affections from their partners does not meet their high expectations, they begin to suspect unfaithfulness in partners. This leads to strained relationships. So if your life number is 1, be realistic and level headed in your expectation of love and affections from your partners.

If you have your life number as 1, you are prone to suffer from physical disorders resulting from imbalance of bile in the body. High blood pressure, spondylitis, heart ailments, hyperacidity, ulcers, bilious fevers, chronic headaches, diseases of the eye, gall bladder problems and indigestion are some of the diseases that may trouble you. Because of bilious constitution, many among you have a ravenous hunger and an inclination for meat and liquor. But these very items are harmful for your health and would be best avoided. Highly seasoned dishes are also likely to bring more harm to your physical system than to other persons. A straightforward advice to you in the matter of diet and health is—take as much water as possible. Curd or yoghurt, fresh fruit juices and green salads are very beneficial for you.

Since Sun is the dominant celestial body that influences your life, you are advised to use such articles or keep such objects whose vibrations are complementary to the vibrations of Sun. Red and yellow objects could always be lucky for you. So next time, if you are going to attend an interview for a job or going to negotiate a business deal, remember to wear a yellow shirt or red pullover. It will do you good. Another means of strengthening the harmonious vibrations of the Sun is to wear the gem called Ruby. Ruby is best worn in the third finger and the gem should be studded in a golden ring.

The number 2: The number 2 symbolises the moon. This number signifies the specific attributes of moon—changeability, a highly emotional nature and a calm and composed disposition. If your life number is 2, it is highly probable you may possess the above attributes. You are charitable and philanthropic minded. A highly emotional nature sometimes makes you very sensitive. You are gifted with a sound imaginative power that gives you excellent artistic talent. You are a peace-loving person and hate to indulge in squabbles and fights. Nor do you like violence for it is against your nature and innate character.

The emotional and artistic bent of mind in you creates profound interest in arts, literature and music. You are adept in concocting stories and in putting two and two together. You are soft natured and can be easily influenced, easily coaxed into anything.

Your greatest quality, perhaps, is that you are diplomatic and can use the power of language to your advantage. You possess a good amount of patience as well as courtesy. At the same time you are kind and benevolent. You are true and lasting in your friendships and are always trustworthy, but many among you are physically frail and cannot stand tough physical conditions. You do neither display false airs nor are boastful of anything. Your simplicity sometimes induces people to scoff at you or to criticize you bitterly. This puts you off but you are so diplomatic that you conceal your resentment. You have a remarkable power to keep your temper under control.

You have a tendency towards over-talkativeness and fabricating stories. Dishing out false information and non-factual stuff can often land you in problems. You are not the type who always calls a spade a spade. Thus there exists in you a tendency to appease, often hoodwink other persons. You should realize that it may be possible to befool one person at some point of time. But it is impossible to befool everybody everytime. So, try to be frank and forthright. It will do much good to your relationships with people around you. Many of you derive pleasure out of mimicry or apeing others. And many among you are born skeptics. Needless to say that these habits have to be curbed to draw maximum benefits through your relationships with other persons.

Number 2 persons have poor sense of dietetics. For you, your taste buds and palate are more important than other factors which means that you tend to care little about what to eat and how much to eat. Dietary indiscretion can, sometimes, cost you dearly and you are liable to develop obesity, catarrh, gastric disorders and similar ailments.

Absence of fixity of ideas is another weak point of your personality. You should realize that too much thinking and too little action never yield excellent results. And more importantly, a well considered decision once taken should be stuck to inspite of all odds. You possess a tendency to change decisions frequently, which tells upon your degree of success in any endeavour.

Another advice to number 2 people—you should avoid being restless and impatient. Because only efforts are in your hands, not the result of efforts.

Lucky days and years: Your lucky days are Sunday, Monday and Wednesday.

In accordance with the simple number 2, all years whose total add up to the number 2 are deemed important and eventful for you. Thus your 2nd, 11th, 20th, 29th, 38th, 47th, 56th, 65th, etc., years are significant in your life from the point of view of important changes, fortunate events and success.

Your lucky numbers are all those numbers whose total adds up to 2. As regards health, yours is a fragile, delicate body. You may be stout but are feeble inside. You are liable to be afflicted by indigestion, hepatitis, anaemia, catarrh, insomnia, excess of sleep, mental ailments like insanity, depression and mania, diarrhoea or pneumonia. In brief your constitution is such that you can suffer from diseases caused by imbalance of water in your body. Your prescription for sound health is a well regulated life in which two things are very important—early to bed and early to rise is the first and regular morning exercise is the second. Meat and eggs may do you more harm than good. You should also take care of personal cleanliness and hygiene so as to prevent infections.

Complementary numbers: You seem to got along harmoniously with persons having life number 1 or 5. Thus while selecting a house or a car or a bride, it would be in your best interest to go in for one with number 1 or 5.

Astrology is a vast science which covers in its ambit the influence of specific gem stones and colours on our life. For you, the lucky gem stone is pearl and lucky colours are white and green. Check out the effect of these colours on your past and present life and you would appreciate the truth behind this aphorism. Wearing the pearl embedded in a silver ring either in the third finger or the little finger shall serve to provide greater stability to your mind and fixity to your thinking.

A word about your love life would not be out of place here. Your highly emotional nature makes you an active lover—both on the emotional and physical planes. You attach as much importance to sex as to emotional love. But avoid making sexual act a regular activity like eating or drinking. Certainly it is not meant to be that!

To sum up, you are the emotional activists of the world. Life without you would be dull, drab, almost vegetable like existence.

The number 3: Number 3 is also the number of creation but it lacks the royal and majestic touch of number 1. This number stands in symbolism for the planet Jupiter and represents the divine qualities and attributes linked with that planet. It represents such sterling qualities as physical and mental discipline, ambition, stead-fastness and determination.

If your life number is 3, you are expected to be a hard task master, courageous, calm and composed, pious, brilliant and respected. You have a philosophical outlook towards life. But, at the same time you are very practical. In short, you are a practicalist philosopher.

The Jupiterian traits in you make you probe deep into any subject. You are adept in dissecting a subject into all its relevant pros and cons. And add to that a lot of patience and stamina—which make you a near ideal worker.

You are a firm believer in God and religion—which makes it rather difficult to find atheists and agnostics among you. Another good quality in you is your regularity of life activities. Regularity and discipline provide the perfect combination for the successful accomplishment of various big and small talks. You are also attracted towards philanthropic and social activities. But the hallmark of your character is that if given a responsibility in any sphere of activity, you discharge it most religiously.

You have a habit of delving into the depth of every matter and taking a well considered decision. Another remarkable quality of yours is a tendency to follow rules and regulations under all circumstances practicable.

But you should understand that being conformist and law-abiding does not mean that you become an egotist. You have a tendency to feel that since you perform all work according to specified norms and regulations, you are a model for others to emulate and develop a heightened sense of self esteem. This is a weak point of your personality. You should try to overcome this tendency as it makes you egoistic, stubborn and fastidious and also sometimes rigid. And mind you, ego breeds anger. You lose your temper frequently and do or say untoward things which make you repent later. Many persons among you arc also afflicted by jealousy and a habit of unduly criticising others. The Jupiterian influence on your mind also sometimes makes a profligate at spending. Excess spending often puts a drain on your monetary resources and occasionally lands you in a tight situation.

In this age of non-conformists, strict adherance to laws and regulation is like treading a sword's edge. And you being a religious law abider and a hard working zealot can easily develop tension of the mind. Some of you try to assuage this tension in liquor and other intoxicants. Excessive indulgence in such things is bound to have a further adverse effect on your mental and physical health.

Lucky Days and Years: Your lucky days are Monday, Tuesday and Thursday. Important and beneficial years for you are all those whose numbers add up to a 3, 12, 21 or 30. Thus your significant years, starting from the 3rd year onwards are as: 12, 21, 30, 39, 48, 57, 66, 75, 84, etc. These years in your life will be marked by important events in regard to wealth, education, profession, family, etc.

On the health front you are liable to suffer from ailments connected with fat metabolism of the body, liver problems, backache or spondylitis, insomnia, rheumatism, gallstones, hyperacidity and gastric ulcers, appendicitis and oedimatous conditions. Most of your ailments stem from overwork, overstrain, curtailment of sleep, and indulgence in rich food and intoxicants. Needless to state that simple food and regulated life-style are the answer to many of your health problems.

Complementary numbers: The numbers 1, 2 and 9 are your complementary numbers. Association with these numbers in any manner or situation will always prove beneficial and lucky for you.

If your life number is 3, you attach greater importance to love and affection rather than sex. Your outlook towards conjugal relationships is mature and that makes your love relationships stable and provides the much needed physical and mental support from the opposite sex. This, however, does not mean that you underplay the sexual part of conjugal life. You tend to keep sex in its rightful place rather than get overwhelmed by passion.

You are the architects of the material world with your depth of thinking and devotion to work. But you must curb the tendency to be profligate with money. You should also avoid overstraining yourself at work. Excess of everything is bad—remember. This adage applies perfectly to you. Setting reasonable limits on every diurnal activity and following a well regulated regimen will go a long way in keeping you physically and mentally fit.

The number 4: Number 4 is an enigmatic, mysterious number. Western Astrologers link this number with the planet Uranus, a trans-Saturnine planet of our solar system that was discovered on 13th March 1781 by William Herschell. Uranus was discovered on 13th day of March and the number 13 also totals up to a 4!

As regards the pristine Hindu Astrology, it does not take into cognizance Uranus. In Hindu Numerology, the number 4 is linked with Rahu, a shadowy planet. In fact Hindu Astrology indicates that effects of Uranus, Neptune and Pluto (and any other planets that may be discovered hereafter) on the earth and the earthlings are fully taken care of by the two shadowy planets—Rahu and Ketu. Without going into further details of the differences between Western and the Hindu Astrology, we come back to our exposition of the number 4.

If your life number is 4, yours is a unique personality. Strangeness, eccentricity, stubbornness, extremes of habit and behavioural traits and great courage and stamina are the hallmarks of your personality. Your life is marked with unexpected turnout of events, frequent changes and lots of ups and downs. Your life cannot exactly be termed fortunate, there are always many obstacles to surmount and many difficulties to overcome. It is a life of struggles. But your indomitable courage and never-say-die attitude sees you through all difficulties. Your thinking, attitudes and decisions also change quickly. Many among you are also given to fits of anger. But your anger is as transitory as your moods and decisions.

You have a remarkable power to digest secrets. Many a secret can remain buried in the vast ocean of your mind until you decide on your own to bring it out. But the wonderful fact is that some of you can be just the opposite of secretive. Some of you are so open-minded that you hate to keep any secret in your mind. Many people with life number 4 are found to be very enthusiastic about a certain matter today, only to become indifferent tomorrow. Sometimes, even these people are surprised at their own changeability of dispositions!

You are often unconventional in your approach to work. And it must be said that many among you are non-conformists. You hate to follow rules and regulations. In societies, groups or associations you attempt to bring new sets of rules and regulations. You have extreme characteristics and you are often extremists. Whether it is intelligence, talent in any field, physical structure or mental traits like honesty or dishonesty, you display characteristics of extreme degree. Uniqueness is often a feature of your personality. Greed is perhaps your weakness. You are really avaricious—especially for money. But reckless pursuit of money can often land you in a mess. Never give in to the temptation of making a fast buck by unscrupulous means. You may be a gainer in the short term. But you'll always be the loser in the long run.

You are straightforward and honest in your dealings with others. And you make good number of friends because of this quality. But frequently, you allow your friends to get too close to you and many of them exploit this naive weakness of yours for their own gains. You are, therefore, advised to observe formality and exercise restraint in your interaction with others in situations which warrant such controlled behaviour. For, others are not so open-minded, sincere and straightforwarded as you are.

You have great qualities of entrepreneurship. For most of you, no work is too difficult. You also know how to make others work for you. In that sense you are a good administrator.

Lucky Days and Years: Your lucky days are Wednesday and Friday; as such you are advised to perform important tasks on these days. Even Saturday is not deemed bad for you. In accordance with the no. 4 series, the years of significance and favourable influence for you are your 4th, 13th, 22nd, 31st, 40th, 49th, 58th, 67th, 76th, etc. years. Look back and see—important or landmark events in your life would have occurred in these years. Your complementary numbers are 5, 6 and 8. Hence you may get along well with people whose life number is 5, 6 or 8.

On the health front, you are susceptible to seasonal ailments, like cough, cold, sinusitis, fever, constipation, rheumatism, etc. Chronic ailments that are likely to afflict you are those caused by excesses of any kind. Avoid excess of sleep, work or even excessive exercise. Avoid laziness. Many people among you are in the habit of day-dreaming and idle brooding. Just give up this habit. Remember, an idle mind is a devil's workshop. Such pieces of advice are necessary for you since many of you have bouts of mental depression and melancholia. The answer to such problem is auto suggestion as also a regulated lifestyle. You are also prone to such diseases as indigestion, earache, gout, blood disorders and problems caused by insect bites and skin affections.

An interesting feature of your health and physical picture is that often you suffer from strange, mysterious ailments which are difficult to diagnose. In such situations, the more drugging you indulge in, the worse your disease grows. For you, the best course is to avoid drugs altogether and follow a natural lifestyle or a naturopathic, drugless course of treatment.

Number 4 people are a different crowd. Because of their uniqueness of personality and unconventionality in many spheres, they are often misunderstood. This explains why they have many enemies and few real friends. There are some other weak points in the character of these people. They are often indecisive and indisciplined. This does not mean that they are necessarily immoral, rather they find it difficult to follow a routinised regimen. Further many of them are outspoken and self centered. If you are also governed by no. 4, its vibrations can induce some of the above characteristics in you but you have the courage, the strong will-power and often the sound moral sense to check such tendencies and steer yourself on the path of progress.

The number 5: The number 5 is symbolic of the planet Mercury. Naturally, it partakes of many characteristics of this planet. If you have your life number as 5, you are likely to be learned, intelligent, clever, good in speech and oratory, a fast friend, humorous, fond of poetry and music or a poet and musician in your own right, patient and composed, benevolent and quick thinking. Mercury is quick-silver and this chemical element possesses some remarkable properties. It takes the shape of the container in which it is poured. It, in fact, rapidly changes its shape. You, no. 5 people have quite a similar character. You are changeable and adjustable. You are very flexible and are considered an easy-to-get along with person in the society. Your sharp mind is capable of thinking and analysing rapidly. This is a great quality in the contemporary world. In this jet age, time is at a great premium. Your quick thinking faculty, is a great asset in any business endeavour.

Your most remarkable quality is your attractive, magnetic personality which attracts and endears people to you. It is unlikely that you may have any real enemies. Not only you are clever and diplomatic, you have a strong friendly disposition even within. No wonder, you have many good friends who benefit you a lot in your life.

You have a commercial approach to life and in all your activities in life. In keeping with the nature of your ruling planet, you have a penchant for profitable gains from business activities that yield quick results and dividends. An example is the share market, speculative trading and similar commercial activity. You love to indulge in such activity and do make good gains therefrom—in a short span of time.

You like to be continuously engrossed and hate to idle away your time. This is an excellent habit which keeps you involved in productive activity. Another remarkable quality of yours is that you can take adversity in your stride. Shocks and jolts affect you but only temporarily. Your remarkable segacity enables you to swim through the currents of life rather smoothly.

You have some weaknesses also. Your overactive mind gives you a tendency to enter or interfere in many different fields of learning or working which makes you a 'jack of all trades and master of none'. In an age of specialisation, this tendency is unlikely to be helpful. You are also suspicious and jealous. These tendencies also pose serious impediments in your success in this material world. Patience is another virtue which is often wanting in you. Excitement, impatience and restlessness frequently prevent you from completing your tasks effectively and efficiently. Try to cultivate patience and equanimity of mind. Try not to be overawed by success and despondent in failure. You will be able to achieve a lot more.

The influence of 'quicksilver' like Mercury on your mind produces an inclination to be over-talkative. Indulgence in gossip is good but only for very brief periods and very occasionally. Remember, gossiping and rumour-mongering are unproductive activities and consume lot of time and energy without producing any tangible output. Put your hyperactive intellect to useful, productive activity and you will realise that you are capable of much more than what people or even you think.

Lucky Days and Years: Your lucky days are Wednesday and Friday. Even Sunday is considered a favourable day. Important years in your life are these which numerically sum up to the number 5. These years are 5th, 14th, 23rd, 32nd, 41st, 50th, 59th, 68th, 77th, 86th, etc.

You seem to get along well with people having life numbers 1 and 6.

In the matter of health and disease, you seem to be susceptible to ailments like nervous debility, epilepsy, ear disorders, nose and throat diseases, intestinal disorders, skin diseases like eczema, diarrhoea and dysentery, oral diseases and mania. What makes you susceptible to such ailments? Your tendency to overuse your physical and mental faculties and worry about everything. Worry, in any case, is unnecessary and can be avoided if you follow the philosophy that man's duty is towards his work, success or failure doesn't lie in his own hands. Also avoid over-straining yourself. Work within your capacity and leave the result to God. Perhaps that is the recipe for your happy and healthy living.

A line or two on your love-life will also be necessary. You are not stable in your love or conjugal relationship. You long for change, for variety of experience. In conservative societies, such tendencies can be very harmful and can spoil your domestic harmony. At the same time you do not like your spouse to have any flings. This double-standard in the matter of sexual escapades is ruinous for your marital happiness and peace. You should realize that marital peace can only be ensured if you set identical code of conduct for yourself and your spouse.

To sum up your character and personality, you are the idea 'sparks' of the society. You are the people who give ideas for solution of complex and intricate problems afflicting the society. You are the source of ingenious, creative and innovative suggestions for the effective accomplishment and improvement of any task at micro or macro levels. Without you around, there will be many workers but no one to initiate any work; there would be lot of wealth but no plans to invest it for optimum returns! This, is the hallmark of your character and personality.

The number 6: The number 6 is governed by the planet Venus. Venus is the planet of beauty, arts and diplomacy, of love and affection, of comforts and conveniences. Your life has special place for all these aspects if your life number is 6. You are active, energetic and have a lot of self-esteem as well as self-confidence. You always appear smart and fresh.

You take a lot of interest in arts and artistic pursuits. You dress-up well and are fond of latest fashions in clothes, shoes, even latest hair-styles! Quite a few persons may be found among you who are maintaining a good collection of decoratives, coins, antique articles, etc. It should not come as a surprise if you find zealous stamp collecting school-children among number 6 persons.

You are fussy about decoration and orderliness. You seem to pay more importance to looks and appeal than to quantity or even intrinsic worth of any article. You crave for comforts and conveniences and are generally fortunate to get them.

By nature you are a peace loving person. You are a person who desires to enjoy every moment of your life. This happy-go-lucky and pleasure seeking approach is the most positive aspect of your character. Because of the constant influence of the benefic Venus, you will always gain substantially from or through womenfolk.

You make excellent hosts. It is for this reason that many of you take up such professions as hoteliering and catering. You work to a plan always. At the same time, you are excellent in dealing with people. You make good friends and your friendship and association are long-lasting. Your endearing nature readily attracts people to you. For that reason, you can be very effective liaison men in business.

You are an extremely sociable person. You love to be surrounded by friends. And indeed you win stable and long-lasting friends. You are fond of birthday celebrations and farewell parties. You create an aura of friendliness and affability wherever you happen to be. Indeed you are a person of many good qualities.

Now let us stop here. Nothing among God's creations is perfect. Nor are you. Your lust and craving for comforts, sex, good clothes, ornaments, rich food creates problems for you. Remember, such frailties run down your energies and undermine your stamina. You easily give in to flattery. This is a great weak spot in your character. You should realize that friends are for healthy social intercourse rather than passing time, sharing jokes and enjoying flattery. And beware! Ogling at outside-beauties is going to make you pay for—in your domestic life. Your Casanova type instinct may play havoc with your conjugal peace.

And then in professions and at workplace also, you are a bit wary of hard work and struggle. Without straining yourself and putting in extra labour in your work, you can never achieve extraordinary results.

Lucky Days and Years: Wednesday, Friday and Saturday are your lucky days. Of these Friday is the best being the week day ruled by your own ruling planet, Venus. For you all those years in your life whose numbers total up to 6 are considered lucky. These years are 6th, 15th, 24th, 33rd, 42nd, 51st, 60th, 69th, 78th, 87th, 96th years. You get along particularly well with those persons whose life numbers are 5, 6 and 8 since the vibrations of these numbers are harmonious with the vibrations of your own life number.

Health and disease: Indeed, you need less advice here than others. Most of you are endowed with a sound physique. You are not likely to be affected by any serious ailment unless you indulge in grave indiscretions in your living—in regard to diet, sexual habits, sleep, exercise, etc. Many of you have an obsession for keeping fit through such exercises as yoga, aerobics and swimming. You are advised to observe moderation in these activities.

In case you violate the laws of nature and indulge in excesses of any kind you predispose yourself to diseases like constipation, oral cavity problems, urinary and bladder infections, sexual inadequacies, diabetes, etc.

Your inability to overcome temptations and frailties of many types brings harmful results. Fortunately, there are means to help you to avoid succumbing to such temptations. One is the use of colours. White is the primary colour governed by your life number 6. So everything that has white colour would be lucky for you. Use white dresses, white caps and white handkerchieves. They will be helpful in the proper accomplishment and coordination of your daily activities. Another such colour is light blue. This colour is also harmonious with your nature and you are advised to use it liberally. The use of the lucky gem diamond is the other means to overcome your mental weaknesses as well as misfortunes of life. Detailed exposition of gem stones and numbers is given separately in this book.

You are, to sum up, the beauty spots of the society. You are the initiators of fashion and style. Without you around, the society will lose its lustre and visual glitter.

The number 7: Number 7 stands in symbolism for the planet Neptune. This correspondence is as per Western Astrology. In Hindu Astrology, however, this number is ruled by the shadowy planet 'Ketu', popularly known as the 'Dragon's Tail'. In consonance with the characteristics of 'Ketu', number 7 ruled subjects are highly ambitious and imaginative by nature.

If you are one of the number 7 ruled people, originality, creativity and frankness in behaviour are the special features of your character. You are frank even to the extent of being straightforward and outspoken. You are philosophical by nature and often display a typical philanthropic attitude in what you do. You are an ardent admirer of beautiful things. The fact that you are sincere and do not mince words attracts people to you and they make good friends. You have another remarkable quality. You are capable of judging others' thoughts. Your ruling planet stands for such phenomena as hypnotism, clairvoyance, telepathy, etc. Naturally, therefore, such phenomena also grip you. Many of you make excellent hypnotists and magicians. You are also fond of travelling and are basically adventurous. But in general you are ambitious, progressive and hard-working. And luck also supports your efforts. You are, therefore, generally, successful in your endeavours. No wonder, number 7 is often referred to as the 'lucky seven' in common parlance and more so in club games like 'Tambola'!

By nature you are a flexible and adjustable person. But you have your weakness and drawbacks of character. Your high degree of excitability and irritability plays down your efforts. You should not take decisions based on emotion. Be more rational and logical in your decisions and actions. You will find a remarkable increase in the level of your success in every sphere. Sometimes, you are also a victim of indecision. Here also, remember that an apparently bad decision taken is often better than no decision taken. Try to eschew a tendency towards laziness and criticising others. Criticising people and things for the sake of criticising is a fruitless exercise. Another special feature of 'Ketu' ruled people is their inclination to attempt big things, megaprojects and big innovative schemes. As long as you make plans and schemes that are in accordance with your capacities and resources, well and good. When you begin to scheme big without checking out on your own capacity to meet the resource needs, you land up in a soup. This is what you are advised to avoid.

Lucky Days and Years: Your life number is 7, hence your important life years are 7th, 16th, 25th, 34th, 43rd, 52nd, 61st, 70th, 79th, 88th et al. Monday and Wednesday are the lucky weekdays for you.

Health and disease: You often are endowed with a robust constitution. But you are liable to suffer such diseases as skin ailments, boils and carbuncles, eczema, infectious diseases like measles and typhoid, asthma, bronchitis and even heart ailments. You are also susceptible to constipation, piles, fissure in anus which can be very irritating conditions for you. Many among you are also liable to contract sexually transmitted diseases. Many others appear to develop nervous ailments. Many number 7 people fall easy prey to intoxicants like liquor and tobacco smoking and find it difficult to get out of the habits of smoking or indulging in drinking at a later stage. For you number 7 people, the best advice is to keep these frailties at arm's length, because you cannot be moderate in indulgence of these things.

Number 7 is a lucky number, no doubt. You are lucky in practically all material affairs of the world. But you are definitely unlucky in one. That affair is love and conjugal life. It is rather rare that you get what you want in love. Many times your feelings of love for the opposite sex are not reciprocated due to one funny reason or the other. Failure in love can make you disgruntled and drive you to a nervous breakdown. But if you stop expecting too much from your partner and develop a sense of sacrifice, you can lead a stable and peaceful married life.

To sum up, number 7 people are sentimental and this characteristic influences all their activities. True, strong emotions can help you to accomplish herculean tasks but emotions can be equally patent roadblocks to progress and success. You are, therefore, strongly advised to keep your emotional balance and think logically before deciding or acting on any issue. You are also advised to exercise restraint in criticism of others. Your life remains productive and progressive only if there are sufficient changes and travels. So choose such professions and avocations which involve travelling and transfers. Cat's Eye is your lucky stone which can be worn embedded in a silver ring in the middle finger. This gem stone is very effective for regulating your emotional nature and aids in warding off evils.

The number 8: Number 8 stands is symbolism for the planet Saturn. Saturn, according to Hindu Astrology is the farthest planet of solar system as reckoned from the earth and exercises specific influences on the earthlings in a steady, slow but sure manner.

If you are a number 8 person, you are likely to be serious,

patient, contented, charitable, industrious, hospitable and submissive. You have that never-say-die attitude and keep on struggling till your goal is reached. According to Hindu Astrology no. 4 and no. 8 people have unique personalities. You are also a person of exceptional qualities which makes your personality unique.

Saturn is considered a planet which bestows revolutionary spirits. If your life number is 8, you are likely to possess a sagacious spirit and sometimes a rebellious nature. You have a habit of thinking deep. The result is that all your actions are effective and productive. You hate to while away time. This is another great quality in you. Since you have a strong, thoughtful nature, it is often difficult to tract your thoughts and intentions. You are also quite ambitious by nature. Your life has its ups and downs. But you are not dogged by setbacks and adversities. You have enormous patience and tolerance. You hate to show off and are anything but exuberant. You may appear to be a rigid person but inwards you are quite tender hearted. You crave for sympathy and affection, which may not always be forthcoming. You are a person who does not like or patronise gimmickery and cheap humour. You are serious at heart but also enjoy humour if it is refined and dignified. You possess originality of thought and creativity of action.

In spite of all the above positive attributes, your shortcomings and deficiencies of character must be mentioned. You easily lead yourself into a state of mental depression and despondency. The influence of Saturn also tends to make you stubborn, skeptic and shy. And there are situations when you find it convenient to manage your affairs by living on borrowed money. This tendency is far from healthy. When you are surrounded by problems or faced with failures, you also tend to become frustrated. Remember, frustration and tension are only states of the mind—they take you away from reality, thus serving no useful purpose whatsoever. Another unhealthy tendency in many of you is to pass off into seclusion and go into your shell, so to say. Finally, the depressing influence of Saturn could make you indolent and compound your existing problems.

Lucky Days and Years: In keeping with the vibrations of your life number 8, the significant and lucky years of your life are—

8th, 17th, 26th, 35th, 44th, 53rd, 62nd, 71st, 80th and 89th years.

Saturday and Wednesday are your lucky days and bring you many opportunities or auspicious news.

Health and disease: Typical Saturnine diseases afflict you. These are Rheumatism, gout, tuberculosis, anaemia, tooth decay, mania and premature ageing. The best advice to you in the matter of health and disease is—regulate your diet and keep tension at bay. Balanced diet with plenty of fruits are your recipe for good health.

In the matter of love and sex, you are affectionate and get an equal amount of love and affection from your partner but you seem to lay too much emphasis on sex. This is bound to have unhealthy repercussions if either your partner's needs differ from yours or your own physical system is unable to cope with a hyperactive sex life. To ward off the evil effects of Saturn, it is advisable, for you to wear the gemstone 'Sapphire'. If worn in the middle finger according to the correct specifications of weight and size, this remarkable gemstone is capable of bestowing happiness, success and prosperity.

Number 8 is a fatalistic number in the opinion of some scholars of occult sciences. It would be in the fitness of things to elaborate on this point. Ruled by Saturn, this number naturally partakes of typical qualities and attributes of this planet. Natives of no. 8 experience the force of destiny in their lives perhaps much more than other people. They are industrious and perform painstaking efforts but results never seem to be commensurate with their efforts in any endeavour. They plan travel in the East and are forced to travel westwards. This phenomena strongly characteristics their entire life. Another remarkable quality of this number is that it tends to elevate its native to high positions of power; authority and fame only to pull them down unceremoniously at a later stage. Their fall is sudden although rise is slow. However no. 8 natives develop great endurance of character and maturity of temperament in the process and these qualities help them to steer their way safely and smoothly through the turbulent ocean of life.

The number 9: Number 9 is ruled by Mars. If you have number 9 as your life number you have that indomitable fighting spirit that makes warriors, crusaders and sports persons. You are a born fighter. You are an epitome of courage and valour. You can never take things lying down. You know how to fight for something that is rightfully yours. Along with courage, one must have stamina to tide over problems and obstacles in any field of endeavour. You have these twin qualities in a large measure. You are brave and venturesome and sometimes sway results in your favour merely because of your courage and risk taking capability.

You do not generally possess an even temper and are given to fits of anger. Losing temper in critical and delicate situations can be very damaging for your interest. But you are often unable to avoid sudden rush of blood and succumb to that fit of rage. You are always inclined to attract the attention of others. You have the desire to be called leaders and pioneers in any field of activity. You have a tendency to find fault with others around and are often suspicious about their motives and intentions. Extra enthusiastic, eager and easily excitable, you have a natural inclination to take up challenges and confront your adversary head on. You are not shy of hard work and are capable of performing in the most trying conditions. You are extremely considerate towards servants and subordinate workers. In addition to this, you are also kind and benevolent. You like to help others out of tight situations. You are prudent in spending and this habit of yours can be easily misunderstood for miserliness. You are farsighted and opportunistic and it pays to be so in today's competitive world. You respect customs and traditions and work towards perpetuating them.

In spite of all above, you have a tendency to be exuberant and pretend what you are not. And this does not help you in your social relationships. You may easily fall prey to intoxicants which may adversely affect your health. Your habit of backbiting is also a negative trait. Another important point merits emphasis here. You are very much inclined to follow conventions and traditions, which often goes against your interest. You must understand that the world around you is not static and you have to adjust to all types of situations and circumstances. You must also eschew undue criticism, violence and harsh speech.

Lucky Days and Years: Sunday, Monday and Tuesday are your lucky days. You should plan important tasks or fix up important engagements for these days. As with other numbers, lucky years of your life are those which add up to 9. Thus 9th, 18th, 27th, 36th, 45th, 54th, 63rd, 72nd and 81st years of life can be said to be significant and harbingers of good luck and material benefits.

Health and disease: You have a sound and sturdy constitution and can take in your stride long and taxing working hours without any ill effects on the body. But, at the same time, you are susceptible to such ailments like fevers, high blood pressure, piles, boils carbuncles, miscarriage etc. You are extremely susceptible to diseases resulting from blood impurities like eczema, boils, etc. Chronic fevers and inflammatory conditions can also afflict you.

In the matter of love, you are given to strong sexual urges and at times uncontrollable passion. You are strongly advised not to become slaves to passion. You seem to attach too much importance to the physical side of love. Remember, love has three different dimensions—emotional, platonic and physical. Wisdom of civilised life suggests that one should always control his /her physical desire to a reasonable extent.

Among lucky gemstones, coral is the gemstone for you. Its remarkable power to regulate the absorption of rays emanating from Mars helps you to control the evil effects of excessive heat with which Mars is associated. It helps to keep your blood pure and your mind calm. It also mitigates the catastrophic or violent influence on you and enables you to achieve better success in your endeavours. Red colour is also lucky for you. Use red apparel and red handkerchieves. Driving a red car may make others accident prone but not you. For you, keeping a red car would result in better vehicular stability and minimise accidents. Incidentally, it must be stated here that you are accident prone. Such advice should, therefore, be helpful for you to avoid catastrophic events.

CHAPTER 5

The Compound Numbers — A Detailed Description

Before proceeding ahead in the study of Numerology it would be desirable to have a detailed look at what are known as compound numbers, a brief account of which has already been provided under Chapter 2.

As already indicated compound numbers are those lying between 10 and 52 with the terminal numbers 10 and 52 included. Interestingly, each compound number has specific character and significations. This chapter is devoted to a detailed description of these characters and significations of various compound numbers.

The number 10: This number is associated with outstanding, unhindered success in every field of endeavour. It represents the Sun which symbolises progress, brilliance, success and fame. In all material or worldly spheres, this number is considered extremely fortunate and a portender of achievements and success.

The number 11: This number represents a sincere and helpful person whose actions benefit his peers but not him. People tend to exploit him for their own selfish gains. As a result that person feels the need of help, support and cooperation for the successful accomplishment of his own tasks. But such cooperation is not easily forthcoming from peers and friends.

Number 11 symbolises a highly emotional nature and a relative lack of courage which hampers progress. Purely from the material standpoint this number is not considered a very fortunate one.

The number 12: This number is also quite unfortunate from the worldly point of view. It represents deceipt and treachery by others. It also indicates constant mental tension and also a life of changes many of which are unfortunate and uncomfortable.

The number 13: This number represents a person who is tormented and oppressed by others. As a result, that person desperately seeks to free himself from these physical and mental clutches. In the process he becomes deviant and cynical. He may even jump the law to have his revenge or to acquire what he thinks is rightfully his. Such a person is not trustworthy. Though he may have power and authority, he is most likely to misuse it.

The number 14: This is a progressive and fortunate number. It represents a devout nature, charitable bent of mind and success, in general. From the worldly viewpoint this is a fortunate number in that it brings success and is considered a 'problem solving' number.

The number 15: This number represents artistic pursuits, a loving and affectionate nature and, above all, a mysterious character. Persons coming under its influences are audacious as well as religious. For worldly events this number symbolises success and happiness.

The number 16: This number indicates vigorous activity and resulting progress. But it also indicates rapid downfall. In short, this number symbolises a brilliant present but a dark future. In other words it indicates an assuredly successful present but the inevitability of doom in later life—which is a highly fatalistic influence.

The number 17: This number represents tremendous amount of will power and hard, dedicated work. The result is that great feats are accomplished by persons strongly responsive to its vibration. Such persons get lots of praise and accolades for their achievements. This number can, therefore, be considered a lucky and fortunate number which brings unfettered success through strong efforts and hard work.

The number 18: This is an unfortunate number from the point of view of worldly success. It indicates a person who indulges in imprudent, rash acts and his actions mostly end in failure and disappointment. It also represents a violent nature, the violence stemming largely from frustration.

The number 19: This number has a magical character. It

indicates destruction of all foes and inimical influences in any task undertaken. Success is, therefore, guaranteed. It is a number of achievements and progress. It indicates fulfilment of worldly desires and happiness. This number appears to have some divine influence which enables its subjects to achieve great success and honour.

The number 20: This number represents achievement of objectives and accomplishment of tasks through steady efforts combined with prudent strategy and innovative ideas. Persons responsive to the vibration of this compound number are 'achievers' in the true sense. Nothing seems to stop them from reaching their goals.

The number 21: Another lucky and fortunate number—this number appears to receive the positive and favourable influence of the planet Jupiter. This number carries benefic influence in its vibrations. It indicates progress, power and authority. It symbolises extremely active, energetic subjects who get the full rewards of their work in whatever sphere of activity they may be.

The number 22: This number represents an industrious and capable person who works and achieves but whose achievements are considerably undermined by his detractors. His weakness lies in his inaction against the detractors. But at a point of time when the harm done crosses a limit, he wakes up to the damage done and scuttles the attempts of his enemies to torpedo his work. This kind of a person is hardworking and achievement oriented but his success is limited by the pulling down factor of his detractors. Such a person is not a real practicalist. He sometimes builds castles in the air and day dreams till dangers surround him from all the four sides.

The number 23: Perhaps the most fortunate compound number for all worldly affairs and matters—this number has some positive divine influence which indicates success without struggle in any activity. It is a 'no problem' number. When considered in relation to future events, it is the most lucky number. It is an automatic insurance against dangers and adversities. It brings grand success in any task or project undertaken.

The number 24: This is another fortunate number. It denotes success achieved through help, cooperation and association with others, particularly of the opposite sex. It is a promise of success provided the subject is reasonably careful and alert against dangers.

The number 25: This number symbolises success achieved through much strife and many struggles perhaps because of very little help from other people in tasks undertaken. Experience of setbacks and observation of others helps the subject to achieve success under the influencc of this number.

The number 26: This is an ominous number and foreshadows failure and ruination of one's plans. It indicates losses through bad partnerships and speculation. It portends disaster brought about by involvement of others.

The number 27: This number represents a subject who is industrious, disciplined and talented. He is not deterred by obstacles and he accomplishes the tasks set before him. It is a number of success and achievement through hard work combined with an intelligent, prudent approach.

The number 28: This number indicates warning about deception and breach of trust by others. Furthermore it also signals constant threat of obstacles and hindrances in the path of success. Many of these obstacles are indeed because of too much open mindedness and a tendency to let out vital, confidential information and important secrets. This number, therefore, represents failure and dejection because of lack of caution and care.

The number 29: Number 29 is not a good number from the worldly point of view. It carries the influence of failure, misery and grief. In many cases these conditions result from deception and treachery by others including members of the opposite sex.

The number 30: This number indicates sound talents and abilities especially on the mental plane. Often this is combined with a high degree of ambition and commensurate efforts. This results in a fair amount of success. But this success is largely due to single minded pursuit of goals and relatively isolated efforts without much cooperation and help from others.

The number 31: This number is characterised by greater degree of loneliness and isolation than the number 30. Subjects strongly under the influence of the number 31 are criticized, misunderstood, ridiculed and scoffed at in their domestic and social life. This leaves them without friends and wellwishers. Life becomes gloomy and projects frustrating for such persons. Thus it can be said that number 31 is far from lucky from the material point of view.

The number 32: Number 32 is a favourable and fortunate number provided the person under its influence avoids too much day dreaming and exercises reasonable amount of caution in his dealings with others. The number tends to make its subjects carefree and optimistic. But these attributes are not enough for material success. Hard work and prudent judgement are essential ingredients of the recipe for success. The number 32 is associated with hard work as well as providential help and promises high success provided the tendency to day dream is curbed and an attitude of cautious, prudent optimism is adopted.

The number 33: This number represents an enterprising person who works his way to success in any task he undertakes. This is a lucky number in that it indicates few obstacles and cooperation from others in the accomplishment of tasks.

The number 34: The number 34 indicates a progressive person who sometimes unwittingly invites troubles for himself by his own foolhardiness or the mischievous acts of others which he carelessly ignores. In general, the number 34 represents a generally successful person who has to face many impediments and counter many obstacles but with grit and determination overcomes them all.

The number 35: This number characterises a naive person which is exploited by others to the hilt and taken undue advantage of. He has to face many ups and downs in his life. He loses a lot through speculation and through hasty, imprudent acts. Lady luck generally does not side with him. Struggling against adversities through his tumultuous life, he becomes morose, indifferent or even cynical.

The number 36: This number represents a zealous person who is as happy in others' success as in his own. He has good power of decision-making, a sound judgement and is ever helpful and friendly. All these human qualities ensure success and bright future for him.

The number 37: This number represents the Sun in success, brilliance and grandeur. It is somewhat similar to the number 10.

Persons strongly under its influence achieve all that life can offer—riches, fame, authority and power.

The number 38: The number 38 is characterised by a person who changes colour like the chameleon. He is given to changeability of disposition and fluctuating moods. Because of such a nature, help or cooperation from others is not forthcoming. This considerably hampers his success in life.

The number 39: This number indicates a person who is capable, determined and industrious. He is not deterred by obstacles and accepts challenges. Luck also helps him. The adage—'fortune favours the brave' seems to fit well on him.

The number 40: A person under the influence of this number is ambitious but his efforts are not commensurate with his high degree of ambition. Inspiration and perspiration both are essential requisites for success. Therefore, the above person is not a model of an achiever. He also indulges in wishful thinking and day dreaming. Sometimes this is combined with a fatalistic approach and belief in destiny rather than efforts. Success for such a person becomes a difficult proposition unless he changes his attitude and gives up indolence and inaction.

The number 41: Subjects of this number have success assured for them. They are blessed with material gains even if they do not work hard. Lady luck is with them all through. Such people benefit a lot through speculation and are able to earn lot of easy money.

The number 42: This number represents a creative person who has a lot of interesting, innovative ideas but is unable to implement them for want of support and cooperation from others.

The number 43: This number gives the indication of a defeatist, an unsuccessful person whose repeated failures have given him a dejected and pessimistic outlook towards life.

The number 44: Another unfortunate number, it gives the indication of a battered, helpless person who is unable to achieve much because of his own efforts; he also does not receive help and favours from others.

The number 45: This number represents a highly talented person who at once commands respect of others on account of his sterling qualities of the head and heart. Persons strongly responsive to the vibrations of this number, therefore, have magnetic personalities and a charismatic image.

The number 46: The number 46 symbolises a down to earth, intelligent and hard working individual with creative talent. His original ideas, creativity and single minded pursuit of his objectives steers him on the path of progress. But, as we all know, the path of progress and success is also slippery and laden with obstacles here and there. At these places, the person stumbles and requires outside help. But when he realizes that this help is not forthcoming he prepares himself for meeting the challenges posed by these obstacles. And he successfully clears all these obstacles.

The number 47: This number is riddled with uncertainties, deception, treachery and unforeseen troubles and dangers. A person who is gripped by the evil vibrations of this number needs to be extremely cautious, prudent and circumspect in his task if he wishes to achieve positive results. Otherwise, this number threatens doom and failure.

The number 48: This number represents a life of many trials, tribulations and challenges and a person who audaciously meets them. He earns accolades from others for his brave efforts. He is liked by his peers and gets respect in the society. In other words, he leads a colourful life from which every other person may get to learn a lesson or two.

The number 49: Occultists symbolise this number by a helpless, tired weakling who trudges a path unsteadily. Perhaps fate has created such a situation that he has to follow a predetermined course of action and undergo untold suffering in the process.

The number 50: A person responsive to the vibrations and influence of this number has success vouchsafed for him if he follows the dictates of his own conscience and acts in accordance with his own judgement rather than follow others' suggestions which are more than likely to be imprudent and ruinous.

The number 51: This number is associated with courage and power. Actions of the defence forces or police are governed by it. The causes for which such actions are called into play are generally noble causes. But this number also represents political murders or assassinations. These acts may also have a noble cause from the assassin's point of view.

The number 52: This number is quite similar in its significations and influence to number 25. It indicates success through help from others and observations of others.

Numbers 53, 54, 55, etc., are similar in character to the numbers 44, 45, 46, etc., respectively. As such independent exposition of their significations and characteristics is uncalled for.

We have now completed the basic description of the compound numbers. The application of this knowledge of compound numbers is important at this point. The compound numbers can suggest the lucky number of house to live in, lucky name, lucky number of car, lucky name of spouse etc. etc. These aspects can be best described by working examples.

Numerologically auspicious name: By assigning numbers to the various alphabets constituting your name in English you can determine the compound number corresponding to your name. The compound number is simply the sum total of these various assigned numbers.

Let us consider the following name KRISHNA KUMAR and assign numerals to the different alphabets.

KRISHNA		KUMAR	
2 2 1 3 5 5 1		2 6 4 1 2	
19	+	15	= 34.

This name partakes of the characteristics of the number 34, which indicates a generally progressive and successful person who has to clear many odds and obstacles because of others' interference in his tasks. Therefore, a person who is given this name at once becomes a 'number 34' person and this compound number markedly influences and controls his achievements, success and failure in his life.

Name of Business Establishment: While launching a new business, the proposed name of the business establishment can also be translated into a compound number which can provide an excellent indication of the degree of auspiciousness of the name. Let us consider the following name.

P A R A M O U N T   E N T E R P R I S E S
8 1 2 1 4 7 6 5 4   5 5 4 5 2 8 2 1 3 5 3
38 + 43 = 81

The total of 38 and 43 is 81 which is equivalent to the compound number of 45. This compound number represents a highly talented person who at once commands respect of others on account of his sterling qualities of the head and heart. Persons strongly responsive to the vibrations of this number have magnetic personality and a charismatic image. This indicates a productive and progressive business enterprise.

Names of person and business establishments can be suitably altered to make them lucky. The alteration may involve minor replacement of specific alphabets or adding prefix or suffix to the names.

Name of prospective spouse or business partner: While choosing partners for matrimony or business again, the name of the prospective partner can be translated into a compound number and its appropriateness can be properly judged.

CHAPTER 6

Gain Number and Loss Number

Numerology as a science of occultism has a wide field of application, perhaps as wide as Astrology itself. Selection of appropriate names and numbers with favourable vibrations and influence on the subject has been discussed in the previous chapter. This chapter takes a look at the application of numerology for determining gain or loss to persons entering into partnerships. The application can be extended to groups of people or institutions entering into partnership or similar associations with other groups or institutions.

Consider the proposed partnership between two individuals named Ram Prakash and Vinod Kumar. We shall apply the knowledge of numerology to ascertain who among the intending partners stands to gain and who stands to lose from the partnership.

The first step in this is to write down the numbers corresponding to the first alphabet of each name.

For Ram Prakash, this number is 2

For Vinod Kumar, the number is 6

Next, we multiply each of the above numbers with 2 to obtain partnership product number for each intending partner. For Ram Prakash, the partnership product number is 2 × 2 = 4.

For Vinod Kumar, the partnership product number is

6 × 2 = 12.

Next step consists in adding the above p.p. numbers to the first alphabet number for each partner. This is done as follows:

6 + 4 = 10 for Ram Prakash
(relational number)

and $12 + 2 = 14$ for Vinod Kumar
(relational number)

Finally, each of the numbers so obtained, viz., 10 and 14 is divided by 8 to obtain a quotient and remainder. It is the remainder number which is of significance.

$10 \div 8 = 1 + 2$ as remainder
$14 \div 8 = 1 + 6$ as remainder

Thus, the remainder number 2 corresponds to the prospective partner Ram Prakash and 6 corresponds to the prospective partner Vinod Kumar. We now observe that the greater of these numbers corresponds to Vinod Kumar and the smaller to Ram Prakash. Accordingly Ram Prakash is the gainer and Vinod Kumar is the loser in any deal or partnership involving the two.

Practical application of the above rule enables us to select auspicious (name of) business partner, employer, business or enterprise, etc. Of course decisions in practical life should be taken on the basis of overt and real factors but counter checking the soundness of that decision numerologically has its own validity and significance.

Relations between competing business houses, between popular groups, between spouses, between officials and subordinates and also between neighbouring countries can be beautifully analysed by application of the above rules. It also enables us to judge hidden meanings and intentions in business deals and association at the various levels, i.e., individual, organizational, state or national level.

Today, the international business is markedly influenced by overt and covert political factors. In the name of peaceful co-existence and human rights, some countries are virtually dictating international business policies to their advantage and to the clear disadvantage of other countries. Today we employ the analytical services of such experts as economists, political Scientists and management consultants to formulate international trade policies. Principles of numerology if used as an adjunct to professional policy-making can certainly help in the formation of more pragmatic sound and successful policy decisions. It would be expedient to furnish a working example before drawing this chapter to a close. Let us consider the working relationship between the two countries China and the United States of America.

China C $3 \times 2 = 6 + 6 = 12 \div 8$ yields remainder 4.
USA U $6 \times 2 = 12 + 3 = 15 \div 8$ yields remainder 7.

It is clear from the above that in any business deal between the two countries, China is the gainer while USA is the loser. And this conclusion is endorsed by the situation in reality. China enjoys a trade surplus with USA. Chinese goods are flooding and increasingly capturing the markets of USA. Software and patent piracy of US designs is rampant in China and there is nothing that the US can do about it, because of political and other reasons!

Therefore, be sure, whether you are a prospective entrepreneur, a national policymaker or a diplomat, the above advice shall come handy to you in all your decisions and tasks!

CHAPTER 7

Numbers and Professions

Generally because of a lack of decision making or self confidence, people are unable to choose their profession. Numbers can help them to take a final decision on this. As already given in the exposition of simple numbers, each number governs certain specific professions.

If your life number is 2, it is advisable for you to select your profession which is in harmony with this number. In fact if you take up a profession ruled by the number 2, these are bright chances of your success, progress and prosperity through this profession. In case, however, you take up a different profession which is not ruled by the number 2, you may have to struggle hard to come up in that profession. Further, you may have to face a lot of unforeseen problems and odd situations which would hamper progress. And your lack of success in such a profession may be in spite of your best efforts and sustained hard work.

Life number 1: This number rules the undermentioned fields of avocation:

- Physicians
- Medical Consultancy
- Service career in the Government, especially administrative service
- Politics
- Business of gems, fruits, foodgrains, agricultural commodities, tea, coffee and other beverages
- Professions connected with copper, gold, sulphur, phosphatic fertilizers

- Professions connected with non-conventional sources of energy, e.g., solar generation, wind power generation, bio-gas power plant, etc.

Life number 2: Professions in the following fields or related to the following items fall under the rulership of the number 2. These are best suited to persons having the life number 2:

- Soft drinks, perfumes, drugs and pharmaceutical products
- Nursing profession
- Professional photography
- Artistry, painting and sculpture
- Dairy industry
- Profession connected with dietetics and nutrition
- Glass items like cutlery, bangles, etc.
- Furniture
- Mineral water
- Navigation and water transport
- Gems and gemstones
- Poetry and philosophy
- Hotels and restaurants.

Life number 3: Since number 3 represents the planet Jupiter, the professions and avocations governed by it are those that involve largely mental work. These professional fields are listed below:

- Legal profession
- Teaching and educational field
- Consultancy and counselling
- Priesthood and religious avocations
- Import and export
- Secretarial work
- Diplomat's work in the national perspective (handling foreign affairs)
- Architecture
- Advertising
- Professions related to time management, e.g., production and marketing of watches, clocks, etc.

Life number 4: This number is influenced by the shadowy planet 'Rahu'. Professions ruled by this number, therefore, characteristically are those that involve independent working and not partnerships. The vibrations of this number are thus not conducive to partnership or subordination. Hence a career in service or a business in which there is no independence is unsuitable for persons with life number 4. The following professions are ruled by this number and, therefore, considered suitable for those with life number 4:

- Contracting business
- Electrical and electronics engineering
- Astrological counselling
- Mechanic or electrician
- Car driver, railway engine driver or pilot
- Computer or telephone operator
- Typist and stenographer
- Religious preacher
- Scientist and researcher
- Detective novelist or writer
- Acting and singing.

Life number 5: This number is governed by the planet Mercury. The following professions are most suitable for persons having life number 5:

- Accountancy
- Banking
- Financial consultancy
- Share broking
- Investment counselling
- Publication
- Writing and journalism
- Professional marketing and selling
- Trading and business of chemicals
- Bookseller
- Business of spare parts of various types of machinery
- Librarian
- Service with the Postal and Telegraph Department
- Computer software engineer.

These persons would do well to select such professions which call for routine work and light efforts.

Life number 6: Professions directly connected with aesthetics and arts fall in the domain of number 6 which is ruled by Venus. Let us list out these professions:

- Music and fine arts
- Business of cosmetics
- Dance, dramatics and theatre
- Business relating to ornaments, jewellery, etc.
- Trade of decorative articles, handicrafts, etc.
- Professional artistry and painting
- Modelling
- Textile designing
- Interior decoration
- Business of readymade garments
- Hair cutting saloons and beauty parlours.

Life number 7: The following professions are considered suitable for persons having 7 as their life number:

- Archaeology
- Aviation
- Magic and witchcraft
- Detective services
- Investigative journalism
- Trade of rubber and plastics
- Tourism
- Tourist guide
- Yoga and naturopathic clinical practice
- Writer or preacher on spiritual matters
- Translation services
- Film production and distribution
- Marine engineering and navigation
- Shipbuilding
- Long range communications.

Life number 8: This number is ruled by Saturn and, therefore, all professions and trades falling under the influence of Saturn are ideally suitable for persons with life number 8. Below are indicated names of these professions:

- Insurance business

- Small-scale industry
- Speculative business of commodities
- Sanitation services
- Hawkers and small vendors
- Business of coal, oil and mining
- Poultry farming
- Forestry and horticulture
- Service in national and international welfare organisations
- Business in the field of metals and metallurgy
- Petrochemicals trade
- Commission agent in diverse fields
- Professions related to iron and steel industry.

Life number 9: Number 9 belongs to the planet Mars in its sphere of influence. Mars is considered to represent violence, fights, wars, bravery, etc. The following professions belong to the domain of life number 9:

- Police services
- Defence services
- Building material industry
- Paints and varnish industry
- Building contractor
- Land promoters and developers
- Mineral oil industry
- Sports and sports goods industry
- Arms and ammunition industry
- Crackers and explosives industry
- Furniture and wooden articles' business
- Mechanical engineering
- Surgical practice
- Salt and mineral trade.

The various types of professions and avocations indicated under each life number category are certainly not exhaustive for that particular life number. An attempt, however, has been made to cover as many relevant trades as possible.

While applying the premises contained in this chapter towards the judicious selection of profession/trade, it should be borne in mind that successful pursuit of any trade calls for a harmonious blending of the characteristics of that trade and the mental aptitudes of the tradesperson. Numerology, in practice, seeks to achieve exactly this. Another cardinal point in this connection is in regard to sets of numbers which are friendly or harmonious to life number. Thus, if your life number is 2, the numbers 1, 3 and 9 are friendly to your life number. As such professions governed by these three numbers shall also be suitable for you, though to a smaller degree.

CHAPTER 8

Numbers and Choice of City and Country

Through application of this exciting Science of Numerology, we can also decide the fortunate city as well as the fortunate country of residence. The readers will agree that in many cases, it is not possible to alter the country of residence. Even if you are unable to change your country you can draw the maximum mileage and benefit from the power of numbers by a prudent choice of the city of residence and furthermore the name of intra-city, locality and the number of your dwelling unit.

Let us take the case of country. A person named Anthony Roberts has the choice to live in Canada or USA. Let us find out which of these two countries is more suitable for the person named Anthony Roberts. We assign numerals to alphabets contained in the various names.

A N T H O N Y   R O B E R T S
1 5 4 5 7 5 1   2 7 2 5 2 4 3
28 + 25
= 53 which is equivalent to 8

U N I T E D   S T A T E S   O F   A M E R I C A
6 5 1 4 5 4   3 4 1 4 5 3   7 8   1 4 5 2 1 3 1
25   20   15   17
25 + 20 + 15 + 17 = 77 which reduces to 5

C A N A D A
3 1 5 1 41 = 15 which is equivalent to 6

Now the number 6 is friendly to the number 8 whereas the number 5 is neutral to the number 8. In the light of these relationships, we conclude that Canada is a better country to live in for the person named Anthony Roberts.

Next we consider the choice of city for the person. Having decided about Canada as the country by residence, let us see which of the three cities among Ottawa, Montreal and Toronto is best to live in—from the point of view of Numerology.

We write down names and numerals as usual.

OTTAWA

7 4 4 1 6 1 = 23 which reduces to 5

MONTREAL

4 7 5 4 2 5 1 3 = 31 which is equivalent to 4

TORONTO

4 7 2 7 5 4 7 = 36 which is equivalent to 9

Now we examine the relationship between each of the above numbers and the number 8 representing Anthony Roberts

5 is neutral to 8

4 is friendly to 8

9 is inimical to 8

It is surmised from the above that TORONTO is not at all suitable as the city of residence for Anthony Roberts. He can consider residing in either Ottawa or Montreal. Of the two Montreal is more suitable since the number corresponding to Montreal is friendly (and therefore harmonious) with the number corresponding to the person's name.

A table is given in the appendix in which names of important cities of the world and numbers corresponding to these cities are mentioned. This is given in order to provide ready information to the reader who may be interested to determine the choice of the favourable city.

CHAPTER 9

Numbers and Queries

We are all intrigued by doubts, apprehensions, suspense and queries of various types. In numerology we have answers to our queries and questions too.

Imagine yourself in the position of a numerologist. If a person approaches you with a question in his mind about any affair of his life or any other matter, you can provide an answer to his query by applying the techniques of numerology. How is it to be done?

Ask the questioner to put down his question on a piece of paper. Take that written question and assign numerals to various alphabets contained in that question. Then take the sum total of the numbers corresponding to the different words and proceed further as follows. Let us assume the following question has been posed.

Shall	I	succeed	in	this	business?
35133	1	3633554	15	4513	26315533
15	1	29	6	13	28

15 + 1 + 29 + 6 + 13 + 28 = 92

The sum total number is 92.

After having obtained the sum total number proceed as follows.

A. **Questions relating to success and failure.**

In case of questions which relate to success and failure of any endeavour or project, add 34 to the sum total number and divide by 3. If the remainder be 1, success is indicated; if 0 failure is portended. However, if the remainder is 2, some little amount of success is indicated.

B. **Questions relating to profit and loss.**

In such questions, add 42 to the sum total number and divide by 3. If 1 is the remainder, lot of profit is indicated. If 0 remains, loss can be expected. If remainder is 2, small profit is indicated.

C. **Questions relating to travels and journeys.**

In case of such questions, add 33 to the sum total number and divide by 3. If the remainder is 1, journey is indicated which will be beneficial. If the remainder be 2, journey is contra-indicated. However, in case the remainder is 0, journey shall be effected but the objective behind the journey shall not be achieved.

D. **Question relating to sex of the unborn child.**

To answer such question, the question sum total number should be divided by 3. If 1 remains, it will be a male child if 2 remains it will be a female child and if 0 remains, miscarriage is the indication.

E. **Questions relating to rise or fall in prices of goods and commodities.**

If such question is posed divide the question's sum total number by 3. If 1 is the remainder, the price of the item in question shall fall; if 2 remains there shall be no change in the price. However, if 0 is the remainder, the price shall rise.

Let us now come back to the example cited earlier in the chapter. The question was related to success or failure. Hence we add 34 to the question's sum total number of 92. We obtain 126 on addition. Let us now divide 126 by 3. Division yields 0 as the remainder. Thus, failure is indicated in the business venture of the questioner.

The readers may wonder at the rationale behind the above rules and their application. Even with the significations of various numbers known, it is still an apparently strange and mysterious phenomena of numerological aphorisms. It is here emphasised that numerology is but a part and parcel of the vast occult Science of Astrology which is itself a mystic science. Many of its rules and aphorisms are beyond the realm of logic and reasoning. But the truth contained in them has stood the test of time averages and has a divine dimension.

Pyramidal query analysis: Western astrologers and numerologists have devised their own system of numerological analysis of queries. This involves a somewhat different technique.

The procedure is as follows:

Ask the questioner to write down his query on a piece of paper. Then the number of alphabets contained in each word forming part of the query is noted and is written below that word. In case the number of alphabets contained in any word exceeds 9, reduce the compound number so obtained to a simple number. Then the array of numbers that results is built up into a 'pyramid' type structure. To do this, add the adjoining numbers in the array and write below them their sum. We shall obtain two arrays or rows. Continue this process till only one number remains in place of any array. That number is to be examined for the purpose of furnishing answer to the query.

Let us go back to our earlier question and try to perform its pyramidal analysis.

Shall I succeed in this business?
5 1 7 2 4 8

We write the above numbers under various words.

5 1 7 2 4 8

6 8 9 6 3

5 8 6 9

4 5 6

9 2

2

We find that in the final analysis we obtain the number 92 (in the penultimate step) which is exactly the same as the sum total number of the question in the earlier procedure—which testifies to the remarkable veracity of these techniques. In the final step, however, we have to reduce this compound number 92 to the equivalent simple number 2 and then read the indications given by number 2.

The indications given by the various numbers are described below:

Number 1: It indicates help and cooperation from others and success in general.

Number 2: This number gives the indication of uncertainties, obstacles and failures. Hence, it is not a successful number in the context of this analysis.

Number 3: Number 3 portends progress and success. It is indicative of growth and good fortune. It is, therefore, a lucky number in the present context.

Number 4: This number foreshadows troubles, obstacles and difficulties. It cannot be termed fortunate at all.

Number 5: In the present context, this number portends success through suitable efforts. In general, it is deemed a lucky number.

Number 6: This number indicates excellent success and mental cheer. The success is helped by cooperation from others.

Number 7: This number brings lot of problems to solve and obstacles to surmount in the execution of any task. However, this number also carries with it courage, grit and determination to achieve success by defeating all odds. And success comes eventually.

Number 8: This number also indicates many troubles and lot of opposition to any task planned and/or undertaken. The defeating forces are always too severe for fruition of the task.

Number 9: This number indicates an assurance of success; provided courage and determination is not lost in pursuit of the goals.

While referring to the above descriptions it should always be remembered that the same are strictly in the context of query analysis. They do not necessarily have a generalised implication.

CHAPTER 10

Numerology for Predictions — Yearwise to Hourwise

By applying the Principles of Numerology, it is possible to work out general and specific prediction of events over any calendar year. The important thing in this context is determination of year number for the individual subject. This year number is worked out as follows:

Year number = Life number + Calendar year number

Assume that a person was born on 4th September, 1956 and we have to formulate prediction for the year 1996 for that person. Then, the individual year number for that person is

= Life number + Calendar year number corresponding to 1996

As per procedure already described earlier in this book, life number for the above person is 4. The calendar year number for 1996 is 1+9+9+6 = 25 which is equivalent to 7.

Thus, the individual year number = 4 + 7 = 11 which is equivalent to number 2. Thus, in the year 1996, the above person shall be under the strongest influence of number 2. An important thing to be noted in this context is that number 2 is not friendly and compatible with number 4. Therefore, in many ways, the year 1996 is not going to be favourable and lucky year for the person in question.

The next point that arises is the various aspects or areas in which the influence of a particular year is expected to be fortunate or otherwise. For this re-examine the individual year number and again unfold and elaborate its various significations. In the given example, we list out the significations of the number 2 which is ruled by Moon.

Significations of number 2

- Changes and changeability
- Emotions and mind
- Home and domestic affairs
- Diplomacy
- Imagination
- Arts and artistry, painting and sculpture
- Silver
- Milk
- Water
- Catarrh, indigestion, anaemia and other blood disorders
- Pearls
- Nutrition and diet
- Hotels and restaurants
- Navigation and water transport
- Professional photography
- Gems and gemmology.

The above list is by no means exhaustive.

Now we consider the life number 4 and its ruling planet which is Rahu. We know in what manner or with what modus operandi Rahu afflicts its enemy Moon. We know from the basic knowledge of Astrology that Rahu periodically eclipses the Moon. Rahu's banal effects on mind tends to induce indecision, duality, suspiciousness and wild imagination. It also tends to disturb peace of mind. This helps us to infer that in 1996, the person is likely to experience above peculiar states of mind which may result in clouding of vision, hasty and injudicious decisions and indiscreet actions with harmful results. Next consider another trait of Rahu—opulence. Matching this trait with a specific signification of number 2, say nutrition and diet suggests that dietary indiscretions during the year are more than likely to lead to diseases like catarrh and indigestion. In a similar way other traits of Rahu can be linked with the significations of number 2 and predictive inferences can be arrived at.

Monthwise predictions: Individual year number enables us to make gross predictions relevant to a particular calendar year. The precepts of numerology can also be scientifically extended towards formulating monthwise predictions in a particular year.

The first step in the monthwise prediction is the determination of month number. Work out this number as follows:

Month number = Individual year number + serial number of the month running in the current year of life

Let us consider the same example as given previously.

Subject, date of birth 4-9-1956. Let us suppose that the subject is passing through 1997. He begins the 42nd year of his life on 5-9-1997. If we are to determine the prediction for December 1997, we note that serial number of Dec. 1997 as reckoned from September being the first month of 42nd year is 4.

Then month number = 8 + 4 = 6.

The number so obtained i.e. 5 is ruled by the planet Mercury. The characteristics and significations of number 5 (or of the planet Mercury) have to be linked with similar significations of number 2 and predictive inferences arrived at. We at once observe that Mercury is not reciprocally friendly to Moon and accordingly number 5 and no. 2 are not on reciprocally friendly terms. As such success, and fruitful culmination of efforts are only partially indicated during the month of December, 1997.

Daywise predictions: Numerology also lends itself to predictions for specific days in a particular month. For this it is necessary to understand which number influences a particular day and the relationship of this number with the individual year number and month number. Such number which holds influence over a particular day may be termed as the day number.

How to calculate the day number? The following relation defines the method of calculating day number.

Day number = Month number + date + serial number of the weekday on this date.

The serial numbers of the weekdays are indicated below:

Sunday	1
Monday	2
Tuesday	3
Wednesday	4
Thursday	5
Friday	6

Saturday 7

The procedure is again illustrated by a working example.

Let us suppose we have to determine the day number for 1st September being a Friday for the same individual as in the previous example.

Then day number = 6 + 1 + 6 = 13

which reduces to the number 4.

Now number 4 is the same as the life number for the given individual. This number can be considered lucky and fortunate but portends, fatalistic tendencies of events on the particular date.

Day number holds maximum significance for all events falling on that particular day. But an important point to remember in this connection is the relationship of day number to the month number corresponding to the ongoing month. Day number would be indicative of beneficial results only if it be friendly to both life number and the month number.

Hourly prediction: Astrology and its offshoot numerology covers a wide spectrum of the various facets of human life and the possibility of prediction covers an equally wide time-frame. Considering this, it would not be surprising if it is stated that numerology lends itself to hourly predictions also—and to an equal degree of accuracy! A day consisting of 24 hours is divided into hourly ruling periods of planets in a specific sequence. On Saturday, the first hour following sunrise is assigned to Saturn, the second hour to Jupiter, third to Mars, fourth to Sun, fifth to Venus, sixth to Mercury and the seventh to Moon. The eighth hour is again assigned to Saturn, Jupiter, etc., in the same sequence. After the completion of 24 hours, the 25th hour which corresponds to first hour of the second day is assigned to Sun, since the next day of the week is Sunday and the first hour of a day is assigned to planet which rules that day, the second hour to Venus, the third to Mercury, etc.

Having assigned various hours of the day to various planets, we come next to the matter of prediction. For this, we take the help of what is known as the 'Ascendant number' a brief description of which has already been given in Chapter 3. The next step is to match the number corresponding to the hour in question with the ascendant number. Number corresponding to the hour is that number which represents the planet to which that hour is assigned, for example, if it be Saturn then this number is 8, if Sun the number is 1 and so on. How is this matching to be done? Examine whether the two numbers are friendly, neutral or inimical to each other. Accordingly predictive inference can be drawn keeping in view also the natural significations of the matched numbers.

CHAPTER 11

Numerology and Partnerships

Numerology is a complete occult science from the point of view of its scope and applications. It would, therefore, not be incorrect to say that practically all aspects of human life can be analysed through it. Partnership is an extremely important aspect of an individual's life. When we talk of 'partnerships', we refer to partnerships of various kinds—business partnership, marital partnership or partnership in any other functional activity.

As far as business partnership is concerned, some light has already been thrown on this matter in Chapter 14. Here a more detailed exposition of this subject is presented. We shall begin with the more important subject of marital partnership and conjugal compatibility.

Marital partnership: Numerology enables us to understand whether or not two individuals can make a happy and successful married couple. Let us see how. Conjugal compatibility has two aspects—physical compatibility and mental compatibility. Both compatibilities are attached a lot of significance in societies of European origin. In contemporary European or American societies, it is usual for young boys and girls to live together for some time before getting married to each other. This gives them chance to see whether their nature and temperament suit each other and also whether they make good bed-partners. This type of practice, however, does not prevail in the more conservative societies in India, China, Japan or the Middle-East countries.

The beauty of numerology is that it enables us to see what is materially non-observable. There are many aspects of an individual's personality which lie obscured and are difficult to judge from outside. Numerology reveals them to us. As the present work on numerology is largely focussed around the precepts and premises contained in the Oriental Hindu Astrology, a detailed account of the relevant numerological techniques shall be given here.

The age-old practice of checking marital compatibility in the Hindu society involves a thorough horoscope-matching exercise by the traditional priest or astrologer. Marital compatibility between prospective bride and the groom can be equally well ascertained through the techniques of numerology. Nature, habits, character and physical and mental traits are the attributes of the prospective bride and groom which are matched. This matching is considered very important and crucial to settlement of marriage. This practice naturally, therefore, possesses strong traditional roots. Individuals in the Western societies may wonder how successful and stable marriages can result in India only on the basis of traditional horoscope matching or its parallel, numerological match-making. The reasons, as stated above, are that this practice is holistic and covers the complete horizon of physical and mental traits of the bride and groom to be. Short meeting or dating does not lend itself to such subtle comparison and compatibility analysis.

There are two numbers which are important in this regard—Ascendant number and Name number. Regarding ascendant number, reference may be made to Chapter 3, which provides the definition and significance of this number. Once the ascendant numbers of the prospective bride and groom have been determined, these numbers have to be matched for compatibility. This is done by examining whether the two numbers are friendly, neutral or inimical to each other. The relationship between two numbers from the point of view of compatibility can be tabulated as follows:

It is the practical application of the above rules which is really important. To illustrate the rules, let us consider the proposed match of two individuals say Ashok (prospective groom) and Reena (prospective bride).

Table I. Relationship/Compatibility

	Ascendant Number	*Good*	*Fair*	*Poor*
	1,3,9	1,3,9	2,5,7	4,6,8
Boy	2,5,7	2,5,7	1,3,9	4,6,8
	4,6,8	4,6,8	2,5,7	1,3,9

Girl

Suppose that the ascendant of Ashok is Aries as determined on the basis of his birth date and the ascendant sign of Reena is Taurus as per her birth date. Then, the ascendant number of Ashok is 9 and that of Reena is 6. Now we refer to the compatibility table, which gives the ascendant numbers of the boy in the first vertical column and the ascendant numbers of the girl in the horizontal rows.

Comparing 9 (ascendant number of the boy) with 6 (ascendant number of the girl), we find that poor compatibility is indicated. Therefore, purely from the numerological viewpoint, the matrimonial alliance between Ashok and Reena is not recommended.

Compatibility analysis of marital candidates does not end here. The second part of this is comparison of names. Numerologically this is brought about by translating names into numbers and then comparing them to determine the type of relationship. The relationship is determined in accordance with the following table:

Table II. Compatibility Analysis

Name number of girl / *Name number of boy*	*1*	*2*	*3*	*4*	*5*	*6*	*7*	*8*	*9*
1	G	G	G	P	F	P	P	P	G
2	G	G	F	P	G	F	P	F	F
3	G	G	G	F	P	P	F	F	G
4	P	P	F	G	G	G	P	G	P
5	G	P	F	G	G	G	G	F	F
6	P	P	F	G	G	G	F	G	F
7	P	P	F	P	G	G	G	G	P
8	P	P	F	G	G	G	F	G	P
9	G	G	G	P	P	F	P	F	G

G—Good, F—Fair, P—Poor

The above mentioned letters G, F and P indicate the degree of compatibility between the boy and the girl from the point of view of matrimonial settlement.

Illustrations: Let us illustrate the above technique through a practical example. We take the case of comparison of Amit (boy) with Nina (girl). We first write the number equivalent of the two names.

AMIT

1 + 4 + 1 + 4 = 10 which is equivalent to 1.

NINA

5 + 1 + 5 + 1 = 12 which is equivalent to 3.

The compatibility between the numbers 1 and 3 is 'Good' which indicates that matrimonial alliance between Amit and Nina is auspicious. Another example of above compatibility analysis is provided hereunder.

Robert (prospective groom) and Gloria (prospective bride).

ROBERT

2 + 7 + 2 + 5 + 2 + 4 = 22 which reduces to 4

GLORIA

3 + 3 + 7 + 2 + 1 + 1 = 17 which reduces to 8.

Numbers 4 and 8 relate well with each other as indicated by 'Good' compatibility in the Compatibility Table. Therefore, we can confidently presume that Robert and Gloria are also potentially successful marriage candidates.

Partnerships of other types (business partnership, partnerships in educational projects, political partnerships etc.) have their own importance in human society. The basic factor of analysis in all these types of partnership is numerological compatibility which is judged through the application of Table II. However, for a subtler judgement, numerological gain-loss analysis as described in Chapter 6 should be undertaken. This applies, naturally, only to such partnerships which involve monetary transaction.

For the sake of explanation and elucidation, we furnish two practical examples illustrating the analytical technique.

Example 1: Let us suppose two persons named Anil Kumar and Sandeep Sharma propose to enter into a business partnership.

Referring to Chapter 6, we first apply the technique of determining gain number and loss number.

Name	*Number corresponding to first alphabet*
Anil Kumar	1
Sandeep Sharma	3

Next we determine the partnership product numbers as below:

	Partnership product number
Anil Kumar	$1 \times 2 = 2$
Sandeep Sharma	$3 \times 2 = 6$

Then we determine relational number

	Relational number
Anil Kumar	$2 \times 3 = 6$
Sandeep Sharma	$6 \times 1 = 6$

Next we divide the above relational numbers by 8. The quotient is 0 and remainder 6 in each case.

The final remainder number corresponding to both Anil Kumar and Sandeep Sharma is 6.

As both Anil Kumar and Sandeep Sharma obtain number 6, neither of them is the larger gainer. In other words, the partnership between the two is likely to benefit both to the same degree; hence it is an ideal partnership.

Let us now determine the name numbers of the above two individuals.

A N I L K U M A R
1 + 4 + 1 + 3 2 + 6 + 4 + 1 + 2
9 15

9 and 15 add to 24 which reduces to 6.

S A N D E E P S H A R M A
3 + 1 + 5 + 4 + 5 + 5 + 8 3 + 5 + 1 + 2 + 4 + 1
31 16

Now 31 and 16 add up to 47 which reduces to the simple number 2.

Referring to the Compatibility Analysis Table II, we observe that compatibility of numbers 2 and 6 is Fair/Poor. Thus, the general compatibility between the above two persons is not good. This indicates that at the personal level, compatibility is not good but purely from the point of view of business partnership, the two persons are ideally suited to each other. The two analyses have, therefore, to be considered in the general perspective and an inference drawn in the context of the specific area of query.

Example 2: Let us now consider another example. Taking the case of the following two individuals, we attempt to determine whether they will make good political allies.

RAMESH AHUJA and RAGHAV SHETTY

Here, it makes sense to determine relational compatibility of only name numbers corresponding to the two individuals. We proceed to determine the name numbers.

R A M E S H   A H U J A
2 + 1 + 4 + 5 + 3 + 5   1 + 5 + 6 + 1 + 1
20 + 14
= 34 which reduces to the simple number 7.

R A G H A V   S H E T T Y
2 + 1 + 3 + 5 + 1 + 6   3 + 5 + 5 + 4 + 4 + 1
18 + 22
= 40 which reduces to the simple number 4.

Numbers 4 and 7 possess 'Poor' compatibility. It follows from this observation that Ramesh Ahuja and Raghav Shetty shall make poor associates in any political activity or on any common political platform.

CHAPTER 12

Importance of the Birth Number

In the preceding nineteen chapters an attempt has been made to explain the characteristics and significations of simple and compound numbers and render on account of the techniques of interpreting and applying numbers for the purpose of occult studies. Various different numbers pertaining to a human individual were defined and described. These included Birth number, Universality number, Fortune number, Complete number, Ascendant number and Life number. As was indicated earlier, the most important numbers that influence an individual's life are birth number and life number. But whereas life number is more pervasive in its influence, the birth number is more specific and sometimes a better and easier-to-apply indicator of life events.

Occult scientists and numerologists have given lot of importance to the birth number of an individual primarily because it is unalterable and because it carries a most focused, specific and sharp influence on the native. Keeping this in view, below are given the general characteristics and points of occult significance for the natives of various birth numbers.

Number 1: A person born on the 1st date of any month is likely to be a steadfast and strong willed person. He possesses leadership qualities. He is exuberant and full of vanity. He likes to keep others under his control and often attempts to force his ideas on others.

Number 2: A happy-go-lucky and peace-loving person, who dislikes solitude. He likes to be surrounded by friends. But at the same time he is averse to artificialities of life. He is turned off by urban concrete jungles and loves to spent time in natural surroundings of the countryside. He craves for unattached love and unselfish affections.

Number 3: A number 3 born person is a person of strong likes and dislikes and almost unshakeable opinions. He tries and often successfully to impose his opinions upon others. He is strongly ambitious and progressive at the same time. Many number 3 persons make excellent artists of the stage or cinema.

Number 4: A person of birth number 4 has a distinct personality in as much as he can be made out from the crowd. Most of the number 4 persons have some peculiarities of character and find it difficult to understand themselves or to be understood. Their life is marked by strange vicissitudes of events. But one thing can be said with certainty about them. Almost all of them are strongly enterprising and have excellent business acumen.

Number 5: The number 5 person has a magnetic personality and is adept in the subtle art of making friends. He has few enemies, if any. He lives on his nerves and is easily excitable. He is often swayed by superficialities of life which works to his detriment. An excess of nervous energy in him makes him intelligent and critical but also makes him skeptic and suspicious.

Number 6: Number 6 persons are zealous. Individuals who have a zest for living. They love life with all its shades. They are romantic by nature but in worldly affairs they are very practical. They have a wide circle of friends and they enjoy hosting parties for relatives and friends. They also take interest in creative arts like music, painting and photography.

Number 7: Number 7 is a favourite number of gamblers and regular visitors to the Casino. The 'lucky 7', this number is popularly associated with speculative luck. This belief is not without basis. This number as the birth number of an individual, is indeed a symbol of consistent good luck in all endeavours of life. Number 7 people are distinctly lucky. By nature they are inquisitive and philosophical. They possess a strange power to read others' thoughts. They have a strong sense of intuition and clairvoyance. They make excellent researchers and scientists.

Number 8: Number 8 symbolises the chain of fatalaties on the material plane. Remember, it is one of the two numbers 4 and 8 which have been assigned a special place in Hindu numerology. It represents the divine writ behind mundane events. People having 8 as their birth number are extremely talented individuals who achieve great success on many occasions but they have an indifferent and philosophic attitude towards success in general and money in particular.

Number 9: Persons born on 9th day of any month are fond of arts, artistic pursuits and natural splendour. They are quite active and energetic and normally even-tempered unless badly instigated. Once their anger is aroused they are difficult to subdue. Number 9 persons are also zestful and like all good things of life.

Number 10: Number 10 persons are self-oriented by nature. They are self-sufficient and do not like to bank upon outside help for any of their needs. They are original and creative and hate imitation and plagiarism. It is for these reasons that they are advised to go it alone in professional endeavours. Partnerships are not meant for them. But by the own dint of their efforts they are able to achieve considerably. It is a reflection on their innate capability and a high degree of self-confidence.

Number 11: Number 11 persons are highly emotional and live in the world of dreams. This comes in the way of success in worldly affairs. In fact, day dreaming is never considered a healthy habit. On the positive side, number 11 persons are sensible, analytical and even-tempered. To obtain greater success, they are advised to become more work-conscious and less emotional. They should realize that emotion undermines reason and is a serious impediment to material progress.

Number 12: Number 12 has a strong potency as a birth number. The native of this number has a well developed artistic sense and strong will power. These qualities, if suitably exploited enable the native to achieve considerable success in artistic pursuits like music, acting, painting, etc. Number 12 persons are excellent showmen and perform very well in the field of advertising. They have a good sense of fashion and style and can be equally good as fashion designers and interior decorators.

Number 13: Number 13 persons are decidedly capable managers and executives. In executing a plan to perfection, they exhibit remarkable ability. They, however, are not good conceptualisers. Their highly emotional nature and tender heartedness also often comes in the way of their progress. But if this strongly emotional and passionate nature is constructively utilised, it can work wonders.

Number 14: Persons born on the 14th day of any month like changes and novelties. They do not like to set in a groove or to follow a stereotyped life pattern. They crave for changes and the variety of experiences that changes bring. They become excellent marketing professionals or tourists. Another remarkable feature of their life is that they are quite lucky in speculative activities and often gain a lot through speculation. But they also tend to be complacent and carefree in serious matters which may harm their interests.

Number 15: Number 15 persons are men of masses. They are immediately attracted towards philanthropic activities and like to involve themselves in social causes. They have a magnetic personality and attract lot of friends and well-wishers. In any task they undertake or any cause they espouse, they receive great help and cooperation from others. They have a high sense of responsibility and commitment in every worldly role. They love music and painting and sometimes reach remarkable milestones in these creative areas.

Number 16: Number 16 persons are subjected to lot of ups and downs and vicissitudes in life. In fact most of these situations are those where they are faced with trying conditions. And in the face of these trials and tribulations they also find others' cooperation and sympathetic help hard to come by. All this results in failures and disappointments is many endeavours.

Number 17: Number 17 persons are talented and illustrious individuals. They can be termed fortunate in that they get lot of opportunities to exploit their natural talent and are able to use such opportunities to their advantage and benefit. They have a sharp sense of analysis and discrimination, are tenacious and hardworking and reach dizzy heights of achievement in almost every sphere of their activity. They are 'blessed' individuals who find 'lady luck' always supplementing their efforts in every endeavour.

Number 18: The special characteristic of number 18 persons is that they are action-oriented and enterprising. They are not very prudent and have to contend against grave misfortunes on many occasions in life. Whether, or not they are able to defeat these misfortunes, they remain devoted and committed to their work and duty.

Number 19: Number 19 persons are fiercely independent, bold and venturesome. But they tend to lose temper and are unable to control themselves in situations where their ego is injured. They are highly creative and many among them are artistic geniuses. Worldly success for number 19 subjects is often hampered because of their own temperament and untramelled nature. They hate subordination to and interference by others. Nevertheless, their histrionics and strong will enables them to achieve many of their goals.

Number 20: Number 20 persons have a serene temperament and calm disposition. They are good natured and humorous. They are also quite sociable and benefit a lot from their friends and social contacts. They are also generous and always come forward to help others out of messy situations.

Number 21: Characteristically, number 21 persons are born scholars. This may appear to be a sweeping statement but is generally true as its truth is borne out by close, practical observation. Such persons are progressive by nature and do well as teachers and professors at the collegiate level. But they have their own weaknesses of character. They are fickle minded and indecisive and this weakness sometimes overshadows their good qualities of being sensible and cultured individuals.

Number 22: Number 22 persons are marked by dichotomy of character. They have, sometimes, a deceptive appearance. They pretend to be what they are not and easily hoodwink others into believing that. But these persons are definitely courageous and enterprising. They are also flirting types and highly passionate by nature.

Number 23: The hallmark of the personality of number 23 persons is its attractive, almost magnetic aura. These persons possess a strong power to attract others. This attractive influence works particularly on members of the opposite sex. Number 23 persons are also clever and opportunistic. Hence they fully exploit their attractive influence over others.

Number 24: Persons born on the 24th day of any month are blessed with riches, comforts and a long life. A remarkable quality of these persons is that they are action-oriented. To many of them, the word lethargy is perhaps alien. Through consistency of efforts, which is innate in them, they can be very successful in money-related businesses like banking, share market operations etc.

Number 25: Number 25 persons are highly sentimental and emotional. To the extent this sentimentalism propels them in the right direction they are successful in their worldly pursuits. But an excess of emotionalism kills logical thinking and this interferes with proper discharge of duties and hampers success. Many number 25 persons have been found to be leading frustrated lives resulting from habitual fretting and fuming or from repeated failures.

Number 26: Number 26 persons are either born with a silver spoon in their mouth or have all kinds of bright opportunities thrown at them in the course of their life. They make full use of these opportunities and earn a lot of wealth, name and fame. They become top notch businessmen or shine in the world of films as popular cinestars.

Number 27: Number 27 individuals are born fighters. They have lot of stamina and mental strength. They can stand big adversities and calamities. And in most of these situations they come out triumphant. They are principled persons who normally do not relish others' interference or even counsel in their personal affairs. They are also extremely resentful of their criticism.

Number 28: Persons who are born on the 28th day of any month are by nature quite sentimental. This tendency of being sentimental or emotional interferes with the proper accomplishment of worldly tasks. Another important feature of their personality is that they are avaricious by nature. These persons are not fortunate in respect of friends, meaning thereby that they receive little help or cooperation from friends and relatives in their lives.

Number 29: Number 29 individuals are idealistic by nature and have a good strength of character. They possess charitable instincts and also excellent leadership qualities. But there are many occasions when they offer to help others in problematic situations but are misunderstood and become the target of censure. This creates feelings of grave dejection and despondency in them.

Number 30: Number 30 persons are hard working and aggressive by nature. They give a good account of themselves not only in stereotyped roles but also in tasks that call for creative talent. Their drawback is that they often tend to be dictatorial and wish to force their opinion and ideas on others. Often they do not succeed in it and end up making a mess of their working relationships with others.

Number 31: All those who are born on the 31st day of any month are considered to be 'born lucky'. Lady luck goes with them in all their worldly pursuits. Perhaps failure is alien to them. They are sincere, honest and trustworthy individuals who would not deceive anyone even in their dreams.

CHAPTER 13

Numerology and Yearly Prediction

In a previous chapter, a brief account was rendered of the techniques of predicting events in specific months and years of the future. Yearly predictions are more important because of the widespread interest in these, expressed by the general population. Realistic prediction of events can enable a person to draw out plans for the year in matters such as business, domestic life, real estate, travel, etc. In the present chapter a detailed and comprehensive explanation of the role of numerology in yearly prediction is being presented.

The concept of individual year number: Individual year number forms the numerological basis for prediction of life events of a person in a particular calendar year. The determination of the individual year number is quite simple. It is the sum total of the life number and the year number in reference to the individual whose yearwise prediction is being attempted. The year number mentioned here is simply the sum total of the numbers in the year, reduced to a simple number. To illustrate the matter, let us take the case of a person born on 25-11-1983. If we are to make prediction of his life events for the year 1998, the individual year number is calculated as follows:

Individual year number

= Life number + Year number corresponding to 1998.

Life number of the above individual is 9.

Year number for 1998 is also 9.

Therefore, the individual year number in the example is 9+9=18 or 9, after simplification. The relationship between the life number and the individual year number shall unfold the prediction for various life affairs and events in the calendar year in question. We shall, in the following paras, analysis each case separately, i.e., friendly, neutral or inimical relationships of individual year number and the life number.

1. A If IY no. is 1 and is friendly to the life number—

In this case, we can safely predict gains from the government, increase in fame and popularity and an overall enhancement of prestige. One may come into limelight for any task or achievement. Political success is also indicated during the year. The year, in general, shall be good for domestic peace and harmony. An excellent year for self employed persons.

B. If IY no. is 1 and it is neutral to the life number—

There are slight problems of minor nature to the health and also in domestic life. Gains in business are only modest. Monetary expenditure is likely to be moderately high.

C. IY no. is 1 but it is inimical to the life number—

This could be an year of your enemies and detractors. There may be conspiracies against you and efforts to harm your interest. There are also possibilities of damage to your property, belongings or physical self from fire. An unfavourable year in the matter of trade, businesses and service.

2. A. If IY no. is 2 and it is friendly to the life number—

You may gain from investments and get extra increments if in service. New ventures in business also get firmly established and start giving regular returns. The year may be attended by profitable, short journeys. The social circle may widen through new links and relationships. The year is particularly good for all domestic affairs. Peace and harmony are vouchsafed for this period in the domestic life.

B. IY no. is 2 and it is neutral to life number—

This could be a year of fluctuating financial fortunes with the net balance sheet only slightly favourable. There is likely to be some problem to the health of one of the family members. This year also portends financial losses because of reckless and foolhardy business and investment decisions; it is a better year for those in service professions.

C. IY no. is 2 and it is inimical to life number—

In this year, expenditure may exceed income and you may have to fall back on your savings to manage the domestic affairs. Needless travel and litigation are also portended. There may be episodes of infections diseases like influenza, dysentery, etc. Strife with peers and also with spouse may mar your peace of mind.

3. A. If IY no. is 3 and it is friendly to the life number—

You will have your desires fulfilled during the year. You will come across with strongly religious people who will profoundly influence you. In all types of professions, this year promises rich rewards. This year enhances your literary and scholarly inclinations. In general, the year promises success and fructification of efforts. A good year for your children in the matter of benefits accruing to and from them.

B. If IY no. is 3 and is neutral to the life member—

The year throws up opportunities for professional advancements but success depends largely on the intensity and quantum of efforts. Hard and systematic work only holds the key to success in every endeavour during this year. Income and expenditure are rather evenly matched in this year. Small gains are indicated from the employer or from kith and kin.

C. If IY no. is 3 and is inimical to the life number—

The year is likely to bring strife and skirmishes with near and dear ones. Like a bolt from the blue, somebody may involve you in litigation and this may be a constant source of tension and anxiety through the year. If in business, raids by Income Tax, Excise or Sales Tax authorities can occur. The worst casually in every case shall be mental peace. On the health front, the adverse vibrations of numbers can result in liver disease or inflammatory affections.

4. A. IY no. is 4 and it is friendly to the life number—

Indeed, the year shall bring windfall gains. Money shall be pouring in from many a source. Business shall flourish. Gains of money from speculative activities may also occur. Success brings accolades, compliments and honour. If aspiring for political positions, success is strongly indicated. You may be catapulted to positions of power and authority. New relationships flourish and you derive material benefits from all of them.

B. If IY no. is 4 but is neutral to the life number—

This year will not give you a smooth sailing in any of your ventures or activities. There will be obstacles and hindrances galore. Problems will crop up quite suddenly from nowhere, taking you by surprise and putting you in a quandary. You will be able to overcome the problems through the dint of your courage and hard work.

C. If IY no. is 4 and is inimical to the life number—

This year will increase your propensities to make fast buck by unscrupulous means. Resorting to low means for making money or for any other material benefit would surely land you in trouble. You may face prosecution and censure. Trusted friends may back-stab you. Problems on domestic front will keep you anxious and tense. The adverse vibration of the year will have its affect even on your health—you may suffer distressing ailments involving intestines or skin.

5. A. In case IY no. is 5 and it is friendly to life number—

The year is likely to bring favourable news and communication. Friends prove to be source of great help in professional as well as domestic matters. It is a year of success in scholarly, intellectual and educational pursuits. It is also a year of fun and entertainment. It would be a lucky year for dealings in the share market. In short it promises to be a colourful year with a variety of pleasant and memorable experiences.

B. If IY no. is 5 and it is neutral to the life number—

This year indicates moderate success on both fronts—profession and domestic life. However, children may be cause of worry. Minor ailments in the form of aches and inflammations may trouble you. Friends shall be helpful and cooperative throughout the period.

C. If IY no. is 5 but it is inimical to the life number—

This is a period to guard against damage from theft, natural calamities and also governmental penalties. You may suffer loss because of strife with kith and kin. Licentious behaviour may also cost you dearly. On the health front, dietary indiscretions may cause ailments connected with nervous system, stomach, intestine and respiratory system.

6. A. If IY no. is 6 and it is friendly to the life number—

In this year, there is excellent progress and advancement on the professional front. Persons in government service surely get promotions and also, in many cases, special awards. The year shall provide opportunities for pleasurable romantic associations. Persons in professions connected with music, theatre, films and other fine arts shall do very well in this year. Achievements and all round well being will keep your spirits elated and confidence high.

B. If IY no. is 6 and it is neutral to the life number—

A lukewarm year in which material benefits are likely to be meagre and deceipt by peers may cause you loss of money. It is, however, an year in which you get better opportunities to work and earn extra income. You would shed laziness and would become more active and energetic.

C. If IY no. is 6 and it is inimical to the life number—

This is likely to be an year of ill health and mental tension. Diseases of the urinary and reproductive organs may affect you. Persons whom you may have trusted for long may turn detractors and harm your interest. Associations with persons of untoward reputation may tarnish your social image. Even in domestic life, peace and happiness may elude you.

7. A. If IY no. is 7 and it is friendly to the life number—

You get new opportunities in profession during the year. This is likely to be an year of real beneficial changes. If in a service career, you may land a better job; if in business you get newer markets and better opportunities for profits and growth. The year shall be marked by sudden acquisition of wealth or unexpected material gains in the form of monetary gains, honour and pleasurable associations. Domestic peace and harmony are also vouchsafed.

B. If IY no. is 7 and it is neutral to the life number—

Material progress is likely to be hampered by unexpected and unforeseen interruptions. There is likely to be a tendency to be indolent and even complacent in various affairs. This may also prune gains and material benefits. New opportunities for earning greater income come up but for one reason or the other these opportunities may not be utilised.

C. If IY no. is 7 and it is inimical to the life number—

This year is going to be a really difficult one. None of your plans may materialise. Unforeseen dangers and impediments may create problems in the fructification of plans and projects. Speculative activities may cause you heavy losses. In business, profits may take a beating and in service, peers may work against you to undermine prospects of promotion. Skin diseases and high fever may trouble you during the year.

8. A. If IY no. is 8 and it is friendly to the life number—

This year is one of patience, perseverance and rewards. Health will also remain good largely because of moderation in eating habits and avoidance of excesses. Hard work will pay in service or in business. The year, more than anything else, will establish the foundation for increase in income and status in the succeeding years.

B. If IY no. is 8 and it is neutral to life number—

This year would bring minor troubles related to health. Treatment of the ailments may sometimes be protracted and expensive. Some disharmony at home is also not ruled out. In general, there may be gloominess and lack of enthusiasm, though financial gains and income may not be poor.

C. If IY no. is 8 and it is inimical to the life number—

A bad year from the point of view of health, wealth and mental peace. Ailments connected with bones, teeth, rectum and sex organs may afflict you. Not a good year at all for real estate investments. It is a bad year for the health of your spouse too. Unnecessary wanderings or travel may have to be performed resulting in wastage of time and money. Professional income also suffers in this year.

9. A. If IY no. is 9 and it is friendly to the life number—

In this year you are likely to remain very active, energetic and enthusiastic. If you take calculated risk, you will be successful in making good amount of money. All real estate investments shall be extremely profitable in this period. Another significant feature of this period is that it will see you victorious in litigation. In general, professions do quite well in this year.

B. If IY no. is 9 and it is neutral to the life number—

Professionally it is a satisfactory year. Minor problems of

health are not ruled out. If in service, promotion could be expected; businesses would do only moderately well. Enemies may try to work against you but their efforts may not succeed.

C. If IY no. is 9 and it is inimical to the life number—

Unfavourable results are portended in the area of business. Services may not do so badly. Health problems of serious nature may crop up. Inflammatory fevers, blood disorders, high blood pressure, etc. may afflict you. Relationship with siblings may not remain smooth. All these adversities may take the toll of your mental peace and happiness.

CHAPTER 14

Numbers and 'Yantras'

By now the reader would have very well appreciated the mystic power of numbers. Numbers convey and control everything. They are the symbols of divine driving force behind every activity. The working of numbers explains past events to a remarkable degree of accuracy. The interplay of numbers controls all present events. Finally it is some specific combination of numbers that determines future too.

As we have seen before, the life number of an individual human being is the most important from the point of view of his life events in totality. It has a comprehensive field of action and influence. In this chapter shall be given an exposition of 'Yantras' (sets of arrayed numbers) and their influences on subjects of various life numbers from 1 to 9.

India is the land of saints and seers. The ancient Indian seers performed intense meditation and spiritual training. As a result their extra sensory faculties were highly developed. They possessed a high level of intuition or 'Sixth Sense'. They were also able to develop clairvoyance and divine vision which enabled them to view past as well as future as if gazing into a mirror. Hindu Astrology as a subject of study was systematised by none other than these great saints and seers. They picked up the aphorisms of occult sciences from the divine scriptures called 'Vedas' and built up the knowledge of numbers for the posterity. They also devised certain 'Yantras' which had mystic powers to influence life events and destiny. Odd and unbelievable it may seen, but it is true that 'Yantras' possess the power to ward off evil, increase prosperity or even bring disaster. In the present chapter is given a detailed account of various types of 'Yantras' which have been known over thousands of years and authenticated by the practitioners and followers of occult sciences.

As mentioned above 'Yantras' possess mysterious, spiritual powers. That probably explains why use of 'Yantras' has become a part of the Indian tradition. Even in this period of scientific developments and high material technology, we find many conservative and even modern thinking Indians adopting various types of 'Yantras' for beneficial effects in life affairs. A detailed description of 'Yantras' in this book becomes necessary because 'Yantras' are based mostly on numbers. In other words, numbers from 0 to 9 are the constituent units of most of the 'Yantras'. It needs to be mentioned here that our saints, seers, ancient scriptural authors, scholars and spiritualists have performed miracles with 'Yantras'. Even today it is possible to perform miracles but that calls for severe austerities. In the remote villages of India, one could come across people practising sorcery and witchcraft and using standardised 'Yantras' for the purpose.

In the context of the present work, 'Yantras' for subjects of life numbers from 1 to 9 are important and are mentioned first.

1. 'Surya Yantra' (Sun Yantra)— This 'Yantra' is diagrammatically depicted below:

6	1	8
7	5	3
2	9	4

Total of each row and column is 15.

Sun is the ruler of number 1. Hence this 'Yantra' is meant for beneficial effects in the lives of persons with life number 1.

2. 'Chandra Yantra' (Moon Yantra): The Moon Yantra is shown below. This is the proper Yantra to be used by natives of life number 2 which is ruled by Moon. Typical physical and mental ailments, losses and setbacks in business and other adversities of fortune can be averted or even reversed through the power of this Yantra.

7	2	9
8	6	4
3	10	5

Moon Yantra

Total of each row and column is 18

(Also called number 18 Yantra)

3. 'Mangal Yantra' (Mars Yantra)—Mars Yantra carries strong influence for persons with life number 9, which is the number ruled by the planet Mars. Number 9 persons are very much prone to ill effects of excess of heat in the body and such ailments like inflammatory fevers, blood disorders, etc. Use of this Yantra acts as a moderating or toning down influence on the excess of heat of number 9 subjects. This Yantra also favourably influences their matters regarding independent business ventures, immovable property and other matters signified by the planet Mars.

8	3	10
9	7	5
4	11	6

Mars Yantra

Total of each row and column is 21.

4. 'Budha Yantra' (Mercury Yantra)— This Yantra, as the name indicates is meant ideally for persons of ruling planet Mercury or life number 5. These persons can successfully ward off the evil effects of adverse vibrations of Mercury through the use of this Yantra. Nervous ailments like vertigo, sciatica, epilepsy, etc., can be effectively tackled by the use of this Yantra. In many cases, this Yantra has also provided its user handsome financial gains from share market and trading business.

9	4	11
10	8	6
5	12	7

Mercury Yantra

Numbers in each row and column total up to 24.

5. 'Guru Yantra' (Jupiter Yantra)— This extremely powerful Yantra acts best on persons with life number 3. Adverse vibrations of number 3 caused by planetary afflictions to Jupiter or its occupation of unfriendly/inimical zodiac sign may bring forth lot of misfortune. And this misfortune may be in the form of ill-health, financial losses or even denial of offspring. In actual experience use of Jupiter Yantra has successfully warded off misfortune and given its subject new hope and a new lease of life.

10	5	12
11	9	7
6	13	8

Jupiter Yantra

Numbers in each row and column total up to 27.

6. 'Shukra Yantra' (Venus Yantra)— This is the appropriate Yantra for use by persons with life number 6. Benefits accruing from the use of this Yantra are again typical to number 6 persons ruled by the planet Venus. Use of this Yantra is helpful in overcoming diseases of the reproductive system and also such ailments as quinsy and tonsillitis, besides mitigating the scourge of chronic diseases like diabetes and urological disorder. Improvement of financial status and increase in overall prosperity also result from proper application of this Yantra.

11	6	13
12	10	8
7	14	9

Venus Yantra

(Note that total of each row and column is the number 30).

7. 'Shani Yantra' (Saturn Yantra)— Number 8 persons are ruled by the planet Saturn. Planet Saturn has its own peculiar attributes and these attributes show themselves in the lives of persons with life number 8. Saturn is a hard task master. It creates obstacles and impediments in the success of plans. Sometimes it brings untold misery to those responding to its adverse vibrations. The beauty of numerology is that through the interplay of numbers, the subject can be made unresponsive to evil planetary vibrations! Yantra of Saturn, an interplay of such numbers is diagrammed below.

12	7	14
13	11	9
8	15	10

Saturn Yantra

(Observe that the total in each row and column is 33)

8. 'Rahu Yantra'— Rahu Yantra was devised by the ancient occult scholars to counteract or mitigate adverse vibrations of number 4, which is ruled by the shadowy planet Rahu. All persons with life number 4 can benefit from the use of this Yantra. It can help them to avoid or 'duck' unforeseen dangers, many of which may be catastrophic. On the positive side, Rahu Yantra is quite capable of enhancing drive, enthusiasm and initiative of number 4 persons and enable them to realize their material goals smoothly. In specific terms, mental ailment is one such problem which defies treatment in the conventional modern medical school but through the use of this Yantra, this ailment gets well. Of course, this does not happen magically or instantaneously; the use of the Yantra only opens out new vistas and brings forth new approaches and opportunities for treatment which helps in successfully overcoming the ailment.

13	8	15
14	12	10
9	16	11

Rahu Yantra

The total of numbers in each row and column is 36.

9. 'Ketu Yantra'— Ketu Yantra is the Yantra corresponding to the number 7, ruled by the other shadowy planet Ketu. All persons with life number 7 are ruled by Ketu and, therefore, use of Ketu Yantra is recommended for all of them for enhancing good fortune and overall prosperity and for warding off evil and misfortune.

14	9	16
15	13	11
10	17	12

Ketu Yantra

Total of each row and column in this array is 39.

The theoretical aspects of Yantras and their field of influence have been rendered above. The practical aspects of Yantra usage i.e. procedure of physically preparing a working Yantra that can be conveniently possessed or worn by the user is now given in the following lines.

The Yantras should be prepared on a special type of paper (*Bhoj Patra*). The ink or medium with which to write the numerals of the Yantra is ideally *Astagandha* but it can be Vermillion (*Sindoor*) or Saffron (*Kesar*). Yantra made out of any of these three media is considered most effective and powerful. The Yantra then can be fitted into a talisman made of gold or copper or silver. The ink/ medium used in the preparation of the Yantra should strictly be used only once. Any remaining or leftover ink should be thrown in a sacred river. The preparation of Yantra should be carried out on an auspicious day and hour in consultation with an experienced and learned astrologer.

There are a few more important things in connection with preparation of the Yantra. Firstly, it should use twig of the pomegranate tree as the pen with which to inscribe the numerals. The Astagandha is the standard medium for inscription of numerals of the Yantra (*Astagandha is a mixture of Agar, Tajer, Saffron (Kesar), Kasturi, Camphor, White Sandal paste, Vermillion and Red Sandal paste*). The Yantra should be threaded with a red string and worn in the neck or on the biceps. Saturn, Rahu and Ketu Yantras should use black thread while all other Yantras should use only red thread. It is important that the preparation of Yantra and all other formalities in connection with wearing of the Yantra be performed on the advice of and in consultation with a qualified astrologer (pandit). There are certain 'mantras' (recitals) pertaining to various planets which are particularly important in conjunction with the wearing of Yantras. All this is best left to a qualified astrologer.

In regard to the Yantras corresponding to various different numbers from 1 to 9, the broader utility and application of Yantras must be mentioned. For example, Rahu Mantra is stated to be suitable for subjects of life no. 4. But it does not imply that this Yantra is not suitable for subjects of other life numbers—those which are friendly/complementary to number 4. Thus, Rahu Yantra could well be used by natives of life numbers 5, 6 and 8, numbers which are friendly to the number 4. But since the numbers 1, 2, 3, 7 and 9 are either unfriendly or inimical to 4, subjects with the former life numbers will only invite trouble and misfortune if they used Rahu Yantra. While beginning the exposition of Yantras, it was mentioned that Yantras are capable of causing as much harm as good and as much misfortune as good fortune. The bad effects of Yantras are particularly severe on persons whose life numbers are inimical to the Yantra's number. That corroborates the suggestion that Yantras should be selected and performed under the guidance of a qualified astrologer.

From here we move on to the other application areas of Yantras. Yantras for achieving favourable results in more specific spheres of life have also been devised and have been extensively used by people in the Indian sub-continent. Even in neighbouring countries of the Indian subcontinent like Afghanistan, Arabian peninsula and South East Asian countries like Malaysia and Sumatra there is strong historical evidence of the usage of Yantras. It would be interesting and worthwhile to present here some such Yantras which have specific, proven effects, if properly used.

1. 'Yantra Chauntisa'— We often seen cases of conjugal discord. The reasons may be many for such a situation—mutual incompatibility, lack of spirit of tolerance and mutual accommodation, adultery and extra-marital affairs and so on. Incidence of divorce is increasing exponentially, more in the so-called developed countries. Numerology can help couples here! Suffice it to say that use of 'Yantra Chauntisa' by either the husband or wife can initiate such changes that will create conditions for re-establishment of conjugal harmony without undue strain on the part of either. The following is the outline of the Yantra which is to be prepared according to the established, standard procedure as detailed in the preceding pages.

9	16	2	7
6	3	13	12
15	10	8	1
4	5	11	14

The sum total of numbers in each row and column is 34 which explains the name given to this Yantra.

2. 'Chaupan Yantra' (General fortune enhancing Yantra)—This Yantra is as shown below. The total of all numbers in any row or column is fifty-four (54). This Yantra must necessarily be prepared by a professional astrologer. Below the numeral block of the Yantra, the astrologer has to inscribe personal particulars of the subject for whom Yantra is required to be prepared.

13	16	19	6
18	7	12	17
8	21	14	11
15	10	8	20

Name Father's name Grandfather's name Subcaste
Birth date Date of preparation of Yantra Zodiac sign of moon at birth

This Yantra has the power of increasing good fortune and gives spectacular results as indicated below:

(i) A person who wears this Yantra ever remains happy and

never suffers defeat.

(ii) Any student wearing this Yantra must pass his examinations and come out with flying colours.

(iii) A sterile woman using this Yantra is able to beget children.

(iv) In many cases poor persons using this Yantra begin to grow rich and have their material desires fulfilled.

(v) Sick people using this Yantra have been observed to recover and grow healthy.

(vi) This Yantra helps towards sudden acquisition of wealth through speculation or lottery.

(vii) This Yantra also has a salutary effect on profession and business and helps them grow well.

3. Yantra for ensuring safety and security of children— The following Yantra is meant for infants and young children. It protects them from all types of evils and dangers.

33	32	27
33	36	37
37	43	67

It may be noted from the above array of numbers in the Yantra that total of numbers in various rows/columns is not the same, unlike in many other Yantras. This is something beyond explanation, steeped as this subject is in mystery.

4. Yantra for fulfilment of desire— The following Yantra is to be prepared on a paper with turmeric. Below the number block of the Yantra is to be written your cherished desire. All this should be done on Sunday at 12.00 noon time. Thereafter, roll the paper on which Yantra was written into a wick and burn it out completely. Do this whole thing on eight successive Sundays. After eight weeks, your cherished desire gets certainly fulfilled.

8	15	2	7
6	3	12	11
14	9	8	1
4	5	10	13

Desire fulfilling Yantra. Notice that each row and column add up to 32. In all probability this Yantra uses the power and vibration of the auspicious and fortunate compound number 32, description of which has already been rendered in a previous chapter.

5. Yantra for successful accomplishment of every project or task— On a certain auspicious day like the full moon day which falls on a Sunday and in consultation with a learned astrologer, this Yantra is to be prepared and worn according to the standard procedure. The Yantra can alternatively be prepared on a day of solar eclipse or lunar eclipse. The Yantra can also be prepared in a locket and the locket, properly threaded, worn in the neck. This Yantra is stated to ensure success in any task or project undertaken. The Yantra is as follows:

7	12	1	14
2	13	8	11
16	3	13	5
9	6	15	4

Interestingly, the total of every row and column in the Yantra is also 34 as in the *'Chauntisa Yantra'*; only difference is that the configuration of numbers in the two Yantras is different.

6. Yantra for kindling devotion for God and for soliciting divine favour— The Yantra indicated below is to be prepared on a 'Bhoja Patra' on one of the days of bright fortnight of the moon and in 'Pushya' nakshatra or asterism. In eight days, 5000 such Yantras have to be prepared and then flown into a river. After properly performing this ritual, the mystic and divine power of the numbers 8, 5000 and the Yantra numbers kindles intense devotion for God and solicits His divine favour for the performer. The Yantra is as drawn below:

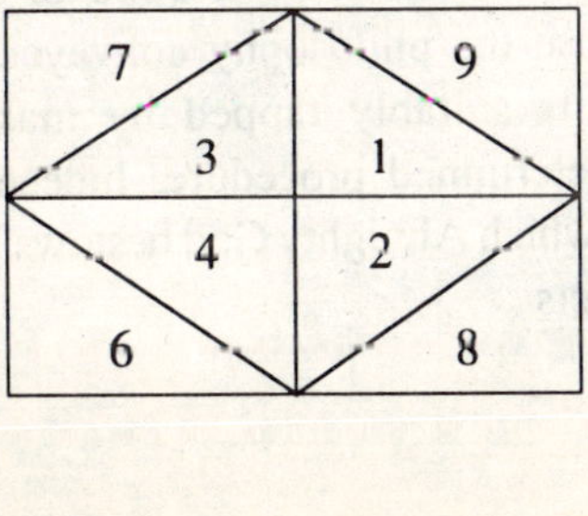

7. Yantra for begetting child— There are many frustrated couples who are unable to beget a child for one reason or the other. The undermentioned Yantra has been stated to possess powers for helping childless couples to beget children. This Yantra has to be prepared in consultation with a qualified astrologer well versed in theory and practice of occult sciences. The Yantra is required to be prepared on a 'Bhoja Patra' with a silver pen. The auspicious day for preparing it is the eleventh day of bright fortnight of the moon. The proper time is 4 a.m. on that day. After writing the Yantra matter in Astragandha ink for 5001 times, the Yantra should be flown into a riverstream. This Yantra then acquires power to bestow issue on the performer. The Yantra matter is drawn below:

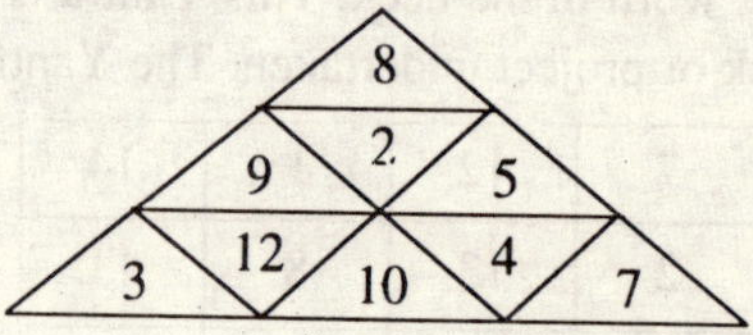

Yantras need to be prepared meticulously. As such it is of utmost necessity that these should be prepared under the guidance of a qualified and experienced astrologer or occult scholar. Any small error is selecting the auspicious time for Yantra making and in preparing the Yantra itself can render the Yantra ineffective. Sometimes the Yantra, if improperly prepared can even cause harm to the subject. Any recital of 'mantras' (scriptural verses) that may form a part of Yantra preparation can only be well performed by a qualified 'Pandit' (Hindu priest) well versed in Sanskrit language and experienced in the use of Yantras.

The curious and intelligent reader would have seen that all Yantras make use of numbers. At some places Yantras have to be worshipped through recital of mantras for fixed number of times. In other case Yantra matter has to be written down over and over again for a specific number of times, be it 5000 or 5001 or any other number. In every case the philosophy conveyed is that the divine power of numbers is suitably tapped by making combinations according to a predetermined procedure. Indeed, numbers are the instruments through which Almighty God bestows his divine blessings on His human subjects.

CHAPTER 15

Numbers in Love, Romance and Marriage

The matter of love, romance and marriage is considered important enough to entail a separate chapter. While giving the exposition of basic numbers 1 to 9 and the traits and characteristics of persons having life numbers 1 to 9, some brief account was provided of the attitudes and lifestyles of persons with life numbers 1 to 9 in the matter of love and romance and in regard to discharge of marital obligations. In another chapter compatibility analysis of two persons was also done and this was extended to the case of persons entering into marriage. However, the subject of love, romance and marriage is for more important and necessitates a more elaborate exposition of numerology and its application in this area. And here we are with it.

In many global societies, especially those in countries like USA, Canada, France, Germany and U.K., pre-marital love and romance is not considered a taboo. Teenaged children freely indulge in dating and have the full experience of love and romance before settling down into marriage. The society can be termed non-conservative in this matter. At many places where Catholicism prevails, the societies can be said to be permissive in the matter of love, romance and pre-marital sex. In the societies of Asian countries like Japan, China, India and South-East Asian countries like Malaysia and Indonesia, more conservatism prevails. Free intermingling of teenaged boys and girls is still viewed with awe and tacit disapproval in India and China among large sections of the population although modernisation is bringing more liberalism and permissiveness.

It is really in the above backdrop that love and romance acquire significance for detailed numerological analysis and application.

Before embarking upon a detailed description of the various aspects of love, romance and marriage in numerological terms, it would be expedient to lay down the distinction among the three purely in the context of numerological analysis. Love is a broader emotion which any human being may harbour towards any other human being of the same or opposite sex. The emotion of love is so broadbased that it jumps all barriers of caste, creed, geographical boundary, etc. Further a person can be in love with animals, birds and plants. Finally, love with invisible and supernatural entities like gods and goddesses is yet another dimension of this emotion. Romance, truly speaking, is just one specific facet of love as an emotion. Romance is love between persons of opposite sex based on physical attraction. The underlying force behind romance is nothing but physical attraction. Romance tends to wither away when physical attraction is lost. Love is unselfish but romance is probably selfish. Romance is based on baser, animal instincts where love exists more in the mental sphere. This much for the philosophies of love and romance.

Coming over to marriage, it is a formal, solemn social institution. Some people give marriage a crude definition by saying that marriage is a partnership contract for legitimising sex. Of course, this definition is of much relevance only in the conservative societies. In permissive societies sex already stands legitimised! Marriage, to be successful and stable calls for great degree of mental and physical adjustment between conjugal partners. And this adjustment, in turn, requires sacrifice and unselfishness. One partner has to shed selfish instincts and merge his individuality into the partnership. Only then can the boat of marital life be steered safely and smoothly. Married life, to be successful, indeed necessitates reasonable degree of sacrifice on the part of both husband and wife. In other words, it is the duty-approach which works towards successful marriage rather than the right-approach. Individual rights may be important in other spheres of human life but it is individual duties which take precedence over rights for successful functioning of all human institutions including, of course, marriage. In this connection, it is considered worthwhile to quote a world famous Indian leader and reformer of the twentieth century. When asked his opinion on protection of human rights in India, he remarked that in India they had no human rights—only human duties. The rights of one were protected in the duties of others. This great person was none other than Mahatma Gandhi, whose life history is numerologically analysed in the next chapter.

For a succinct analysis of love, romance and marriage through the working of numbers, one has to use the standard life number for love and romance and ascendant number in conjunction with name number for judging marriage compatibility. Why? The life number is appropriate as a basis for numerological analysis of love and romance as it takes into account individual attributes, traits and relationships. Marriage is a very specific aspect of life in which absolute individuality of a person counts as much as the environmental aspects. Therefore, both ascendant number and name number are important bases for numerological judgement of marital compatibilities. The individual attitudes and philosophies of marriage are, however, best explained through life number only.

Love and Romance: The subject of love and romance and useful tips based on numerology are discussed below:

Life Number 1: Number 1 subjects are fiercely independent, creative, magnanimous and open-minded. They have excellent qualities of leadership. If your life number is 1, you easily attract persons of the opposite sex and also involve yourself with him or her. You tend to maintain your individuality in your affairs and are inclined to enjoy all aspects of the affair. To you, fulfilment of a relationship lies in your partner completely surrendering to you. You expect full fidelity and faithfulness from your partner. After you have had your enjoyment of the romantic relationship, you tend to feel unsatisfied and vacuous again and look in for fresh involvements. Your love affairs most frequently start with your prospective love partner getting attracted towards you because of your physical charm and magnetic personality. The sheer brilliance of your personality is often enough to draw people to you. But then you tend to be very demanding in love. It is for this reason that many of your love partners desert you as quickly as they fell for you and approached you in the first instance. Sometimes you also unnecessarily suspect your partner of unfaithfulness. This also tells upon your relationships.

You get instinctively attracted towards members of the opposite sex who have life numbers 1, 2, 3 or 5. But your best and most satisfying affair is likely with a person of life number either 2 or 3. The undermentioned table indicates the degree of satisfaction that love affair or romantic relationship would provide you with subjects of various different numbers.

Life Number	*Type and Quality of Relationship*
1	Dull, lustreless but stable and reasonably satisfying, there is likely to be mutual respect for each other's individuality but fulfilment of relationship may be wanting.
2	An interesting relationship, highly satisfying for both, either partner will have experiences that will prove valuable in future life, but too much involvement emotionally may not be in the best interest of the love partners purely from the worldly point of view.
3	Excellent relationship; both partners know each other well and thoroughly understand each other's strengths and frailties; apart from physical attraction and compatibility both have respect and regard for each other which is the hallmark of genuine love.
4	This relationship does not work well; the domineering nature of No. 1 subject is detested by the independent minded No. 4 subject. Mentally and emotionally, quite unmade for each other. Even if there is interaction, there are bound to occur misunderstandings sooner than later.
5	Physically, the relationship is typically one sided i.e. No. 5 subject may be attracted towards No. 1 subject but not vice versa. On a mental plane this could be a more than satisfactory romantic relationship with matching interest in each other's ideas and notions.

6	Unsatisfactory relationship. No. 6 person hankers too much after physical love whereas same is not true of No. 1 person. No. 1 and No. 6 persons are likely to come together only on some false ground and are likely to drift apart sooner than they come together.
7	A very indifferent relationship. Natures and temperaments differ and so do the degree of cravings for physical love. The honest thinking and straightforward approach of No. 1 are in contrast to the erratic, unpredictable and often untoward behaviour of No. 7. It is not a good relationship.
8	A thoroughly unsatisfactory relationship. The royal and majestic style of No. 1 is misunderstood as arrogance by No. 8. The cold rigidity of No. 8 is detested by No. 1 who is warm and affectionate.
9	No. 1 and No. 9 are friendly and compatible numbers; subjects of both are warm, adventurous, curious and active—therefore, their relationship is very good at least on the physical level. Mentally the brute and crude behaviour of No. 9 person may sometimes not vibe well with the dignified behaviour of No. 1 person but, on the whole, they both adjust well with each other mentally and emotionally too.

Number 1 persons should choose their love partners out of those with life numbers 2, 3 and 9. They should try to curb excessive ego and vanity and come to terms of equality and reciprocity with their partners. That will make their affairs truly more satisfying and fulfilling.

Life Number 2: If your life number is 2, you are cool, changeable and highly emotional. You are particularly sentimental in the matter of love and romance. Since others are not likely to be so emotional and sentimental, your intensity of romantic feelings may not be equally shared by your love partner. This may sometimes create imbalance in your love relationships. Another important characteristic is that you tend to lay too much emphasis on faithfulness and emotional love and tend to ignore sex. For you sex is a mechanical activity which you tend to delink from emotional love. You are a purist lover. Your love is not adulterated by any element of selfishness. You are also prepared to sacrifice your interests for the happiness and appeasement of your lover. The intensity and quality of your romantic sentiment is so great that is often transcends established norms, conventions and limits. Your best partners for romance and love are persons with life numbers 1, 3 and 9. Further details of your romantic relationship with other number subjects are given below:

Life Number	*Type and Quality of Relationship*
1	Details of this relationship are the same as given for life No. number 2 - life No. 1 relationship in the foregoing pages.
2	This relationship, again, is somewhat dull in the sense that both partners are highly emotional and unselfish. The affair would be stable and successful but not rich and interesting. In fact, in the first instance only, No. 2 person may be not particularly attracted towards another No. 2 person.
3	Excellent relationship, the two can be very good love partners. The emotive element of no. 2 person fits well with the passionate element of No. 3 person. The relationship strikes the optimum balance of emotion, passion and mutual respect. A most satisfying and enduring relationship.
4	No. 2 persons are highly emotional and faithful whereas their No. 4 partners are given to suspicion. Instability, unpredictability and changeability are the hallmarks of the personality and behaviour of No. 4 person and hence he/she cannot adjust with No. 2 person in the matter of love and romance.
5	It is the low degree of faithfulness and sexual discipline that marks the love habits of No. 5 person who may strike adjustment with the purist lover

	No. 2 person as long as the latter does not become disappointed which he/she is likely to get sooner than later—A low/poor quality relationship.
6	An incompatible and inimical relationship. No. 2 is steadfast in faith whereas No. 6 seeks variety, No. 2 keeps physical desires in check whereas No. 6 leaves them unrestrained.
7	A relationship good in parts. No. 2 persons are stable in love but No. 7 persons are changeable and have an obsession for beauty and art. No. 2 is down to earth but No. 7 is philosophical. To the extent their habits and natures match, the relationship works well, beyond that it breaks off.
8	The opposite natures of No. 2 and No. 8 persons will prevent serious involvement in the first instance and successful affair later. No. 2 is faithful and emotional and would find his hunger for sentimental and unselfish love unappeasable by No. 8 who may be egoistic, withdrawn and sometimes selfish.
9	No. 2 and No. 9 persons vibe well in love and romantic affairs. The intense desire for passion and physical love of No. 9 person are duly fulfilled by his/her No. 2 partner. Number 2 normally tends to play the passive, 'underdog' role in affairs with Number 9. Problems may arise only if No. 2 tends to be active or dominating.

Number 2 persons are advised to be a little more responsive to the physical/sexual needs of their partners. They should avoid to be too sentimental and try to be more pragmatic in love. It goes without saying that they should select love partners out of No. 1, 3 and 9 persons.

Life Number 3: If your life number is 3, you tend to be idealistic in the matter of love. Generally, you are a practical person but in matters of love and romance, many of you deprecate indulgence in physical love without a proper background of mental and emotional love. You often criticize brute animal desire in love relationships. You are, by and large, a thoughtful, balanced person and 'look before you leap'. But you are inclined to make emotional love an essential ingredient of any legitimate involvement with the opposite sex. In all your affairs you display excellent sense of responsibility and duty. In fact it would not be improper to say that you tend to make love affair as something of an academic course-work with all its rules and regulations! Details of your love relationship with subjects of various different life members are given below:

Life Number	*Type and Quality of Relationship*
1	Reference may be made to the write-up in respect of No. 1 - No. 3 relationship. The same description is applicable here.
2	Description same as for No. 2 - No. 3 relationship given before.
3	Number 3 relationship with another number 3 is a very piquant relationship of two idealists. It may be mutually satisfying but it is unlikely to have thrill and adventure. Thus, the relationship tends to be lacking in excitement and thrill.
4	This cannot be termed as a complementary relationship because No. 3 and No. 4 are not exactly friendly numbers. The idealism of No. 3 person simply doesn't go well with the suspiciousness of No. 4 person and also with his obsession with material aspects of the relationship.
5	The quality of relationship with No. 5 persons can be somewhat satisfactory provided No. 5 person refrains from excessive criticism and tries to exercise reasonable discipline in the matter of sex.
6	No good relationship - No. 3 person shall be irritated by his partner going too much after sexual enjoyment. The relationship has hardly any complementary, common binding factors and may break sooner than it takes off.

7	This relationship is fairly satisfactory, thanks to the flexibility and adjustability of no. 3 partner. There are many shades of similarity in the basic natures of No. 3 person and No. 7 person. Therefore, their relationship is often successful in spite of extremely emotional and also highly passionate nature of No. 7 persons.
8	An extremely dull type of relationship bordering on unsuccessful. No. 8 person, being rigid and sometimes lustful cannot adjust with the more platonic and principled number 3 person. As such the relationship can only be termed unsatisfactory.
9	Jupiter and Mars are natural friends, so are their numbers 3 and 9. The passionate and adventurous nature of No. 9 finds good taker in the prudent and adjustable No. 3. Both are very compatible on the mental plane. This relationship can be termed good.

Number 3 persons are advised to be more worldly wise in the matter of love and romance by shedding some of their idealism. They should associate, preferably, with those persons as love-mates who have life number 1 or 2 or 9. They should also be more accommodative in the matter of physical love.

Life Number 4: The most conspicuous characteristic of yours is that you have a most indifferent attitude towards sex. You may abstain from sex for long periods for no apparent reason and you also display the other extreme of passionate and extensive indulgence. You do not take the subject of sex seriously. In love and romance you are inclined to give the greater weightage to emotional or platonic love with the element of sacrifice and unselfishness. In your philosophy of romantic love you would like to give more than demand. In case the other partner is suitably tuned to this behaviour on the mental level, the relationship works well otherwise it goes to pieces. In fact, it would not be inappropriate to say that your conception of true love borders on the divine. However, you are often given to suspicion in love. In the following lines is given brief account of the quality and type of relationship of yours with persons of various life numbers.

Life Number	*Type and Quality of Relationship*
1	Already described before under the account of relationship of No. 1 with No. 4.
2	Already described under the account of relationship of No. 2 with No. 4.
3	Already described while giving the account of relationship of No. 3 with No. 4.
4	Persons of No. 4 are individualistic and often unconventional in their approach and ideas. No. 4 — No. 4 relationship can work on a platonic level but full satisfaction from this affair will always be wanting. The tendency to expect too much from the partner and also suspect may only result in snapping of the relationship.
5	Mercury ruled number 5 persons are adjustable and take on well the odd behaviour, extremist thinking and eccentricities of number 4. Therefore, this relationship is considered quite satisfactory. The only condition for sustained existence of this relationship is that No. 5 should curb his inclination towards too much indulgence in physical love. On a mental plane, this relationship goes quite well.
6	No. 6 persons are fond of art, fashion, style and sex. In a typical affair with No. 4 persons they are able to attract the latter physically. No. 4 partner then finds everything lovable and adorable about the No. 6 person. The relationship is considered very good on mental as well as physical level.
7	No. 4 and No. 7 are not made for each other in the matter of love and romance. Their habits, tastes, propensities etc. are quite different. No. 4 emphasises platonic love whereas No. 7 deemphasises it. No. 4

	sometimes suspects his partner and No. 7 actually indulges in outside flinging!
8	No. 4 person and No. 8 person make excellent love mates and romantic partners. Both seek fulfilment of emotional needs and find it duly in each other. Both are able to sacrifice their interests to meet the needs of their partners. The activeness of No. 4 partner perfectly matches the passiveness of number 8 partner.
9	A mismatch, truly! No. 4 person is too dogmatic and rigid for the passion seeking and overactive No. 9 person. Further the tendency of No. 9 person to indulge in sexual escapades may seriously antagonise the No. 4 partner.

Number 4 persons are advised to choose their love partners from among numbers 5, 6 and 8. When they deliberately wish to carry on an affair with persons of other life numbers or the latter come upon them through the sheer force of destiny, they should tone down or moderate their tendency towards extremes in the matter of love and sex. Only then can stability and fulfilment be achieved in their relationships.

Life Number 5: Number 5 persons characteristically crave for variety in the matter of love and romance. Variety is the spice of life and they firmly believe in this adage, at least in the matter of love relationships. If you are having life number 5 you are changeable to the extent that you seek variety in love. You are also very critical of your partner's needs and propensities. As long as this criticism is positive and healthy, it is well taken but negative criticism is often sneered at. You are very particular about minute details in the matter of romance and sex. And this is your strong, positive attribute. You find it difficult to exercise self-discipline in the matter of sex and that undermines stability of your love relationships. Love for you is often like a one night dream which gets broken at dawn and another such dream follows the next night!

Your relationships with other life number persons are briefly described below:

Life Number	*Type and Quality of Relationship*
1 2 3 4	Already described before.
5	This relationship is not very stable. Tendency to have outside flings on the part of both can result in souring of the relationship. To the extent each one can tolerate the other's escapades the relationship continues. Beyond that it stops.
6	A satisfactory relationship but not of high quality. The habit of No. 5 person to critically evaluate his/her partner can drive the latter crazy. Also at the mental/emotional level, the intensity of No. 6 partner is lower and cannot match the intensity of No. 5 person.
7	Not quite satisfactory; again mismatching occurs in the intensity of emotion of love and romance, No. 7 being too highly romantic. Also the aggressiveness of No. 7 is not to the liking of No. 5.
8	No. 5 and No. 8 are natural friends; their emotional and sexual habits are also complementary and therefore, any relationship between these two numbers is more than likely to be stable and successful.
9	An uncomfortable relationship, largely because of the aggressive passion of No. 9 person and his expectations of total fidelity. Neither the high passion of No. 9 person gets an outlet nor his expectations in regard to faithfulness are fulfilled in this relationship with No. 5 person.

Number 5 persons should be selective in making romance partners and should lay their eyes preferably on persons with life numbers 4, 6 and 8. In other cases, they should curb their habit of excessive criticism and propensity for seeking variety in love.

Life Number 6: If you have 6 as your life number you are innately romantic. You are fond of beauty, fashion, style and also physical love. Many males with life number 6 are casanovas. You easily tend to be attracted towards members of the opposite sex. You place love and sex above many other things in life. A drawback of yours is that you are inclined to change partners after having had enjoyable relationships. This reflects on your lack of steadfastness and faithfulness. Nevertheless you have a colourful romantic personality and without you the world would be much more a dull place.

Your relationships with persons of different life numbers are briefly described below:

Life Number	*Type and Quality of Relationship*
1 2 3 4 5	Already described before.
6	There is lot of fun, frolic and enjoyment in this relationship. But the relationship is short lived because the high intensity romance and physical love wears out fast. A good relationship subject to moderation and some adjustment by the partners.
7	No. 6 person can have fairly satisfactory romance with No. 7 person because of the 'emotional romanticism' of the latter. But the latter is restless, changeable and impetuous and because of these tendencies problems may crop up. Many smooth relationships have been observed between these two life numbers.
8	An excellent relationship, again, No. 8 provides room and accommodation for the No. 6 seeking

	fulfilment in romance and physical love. Beautiful and attractive among No. 8 persons instinctively attract No. 6 persons who are natural connoiseurs of beauty. The natures of No. 6 and No. 8 are also similar in the matter of physical love.
9	Number 6 and number 9 persons vibe well in certain areas and not so well in other areas of love and romance. Both are passionate by nature. But again, both are excessively given to sensual enjoyment and may soon get bored of each other.

The general advice to life number 6 persons is that they should be less fussy about external looks for looks can be deceptive! They should also stop being fastidious about beauty and sex appeal. Beauty, after all, is only skin deep. Giving more importance to cooperation, faithfulness and mutual care shall build more satisfying and enduring relationships.

Life Number 7: You number 7 persons are inveterate romantics. Your intensity of emotional love is great but, very frequently, your romantic love is based on physical attraction and hence the element of endurance is not there in your relationships. In a permissive and free society you could have numerous love-affairs. In this connection the writer is reminded of a 20 year-old girl in Milan (Italy) who met him during his visit to that country. The girl (a No. 7 person) admitted to having 10 boy-friends!

You are, however, restless in love and seek newer experiences. This mars the stability of your relationships. Some of you also display perversions in the matter of love and sex. You tend to seek out of the world experiences while living in the world!

As with other life numbers, your relationships with various life number persons are briefly described below:

Life Number	*Type and Quality of Relationship*
1 2	Already described before.

3 4 5 6	Already described before.
7	No. 7 person can have extremely sound or unsound relationship with another No. 7 person. The two may like each other to a great degree but after a while may get so bored with each other that they part ways. Not a very satisfactory relationship, in general.
8	Natures, habits and temperaments of No. 7 and 8 members do not match. The cold and rigid No. 8 does not respond well to the highly romantic and passionate No. 7. The relationship is far from satisfactory.
9	Here the romantic fervour of No. 7 person gets a good expression and response from the equally passionate No. 9 person. Therefore, the relationship between the two is quite good and more than satisfactory.

Number 7 persons are advised to choose their love partners from No. 1, 2 and 9. They should realize that romantic love has its worldly limitations. They should curb the inclination to have extra flings and also curb their restless nature if they wish to have their love affairs last long.

Life Number 8: You are active and energetic in love. You tend to have high expectations of faithfulness in love. If the same is not forthcoming you are driven to dejection and despair. You are quite capable of breaking off with your partner should you find him/her wanting in fidelity and faithfulness. You seek high degree of sensual enjoyment in your relationship with the opposite sex. Many times you are not frank and forthright in your expressions while dealing with your partner. This can create misunderstandings. When you are in a state of dejection and frustration in love, you may even become abnormal and cynical.

The relationship aspects of life number 8 persons with persons of other life numbers are given below:

Life Number	*Type and Quality of Relationship*
1	Already described.
2	
3	
4	
5	
6	
7	
8	Relationship with No. 8 person may be all right but problems can creep in because of wanting frankness and candid behaviour in love. Physical love has its limitations. If you are blind to these limitations, you will invite trouble for your relationship.
9	Most un-made for each other! No. 8 is shy and No. 9 is too outspoken; No. 8 is seeker of unselfish love while No. 9 is a variety seeker. This relationship hardly ever works well.

Numerological advice for number 8 persons is that, as a general rule they should bear in mind that persons of life No. 4, 5 and 6 only will be suitable for their love relationship. Secondly, they should try to shed unnecessary inhibitions and avoid giving too much importance to sex. They should also avoid becoming too despondent and dejected in love for trivial reasons.

Life Number 9: In the matter of romance and love, you are wildly passionate. If you have a fancy for a prospective love partner, you will have no inhibitions in expressing your love. You will convey your feelings in most unequivocal, candid manner. However, if adequate response is not forthcoming from your partner, you tend to be disturbed and dissatisfied. You are not very flexible in adjusting to the needs and nuances of your partner's love. Also you attach too much importance to the matter of physical love. Further you have a marked tendency to be dominating in your affair. This may be responded to positively or negatively depending upon the nature of your love-partner.

Most of the important points on the nature and type of relationship of No. 9 persons with other number persons have already been covered. However, for the sake of uniformity the table of relationships is again given below:

Life Number	*Type and Quality of Relationship*
1	Already covered
2	
3	
4	
5	
6	
7	
8	
9	The relationship is not dull but short-lived, for attraction of physical love doesn't last long. The short temper and dominating nature of both partners also comes in the way of enduring relationship.

Number 9 persons are strongly advised to control their temper and a tendency to dominate the other partner in romantic relationship. They are also advised not to become slaves to passion and take relationship in a holistic sense.

Numerology in Marriage

The subject of numerologically choosing the most compatible marriage partner has already been touched upon in a previous chapter. The individual's beliefs, attitudes and philosophies on marriage and the manner in which every individual handles married life shall now be discussed. Individuals of life numbers 1 to 9 interact with their life partners and families in varied manner; they also deal with various affairs of domestic life in their own interesting ways. Let us see, how.

Life Number 1: Number 1 likes to boss around. He would like his spouse to follow his instructions in generally all affairs of the family. He is a spendthrift and floods his spouse and children with all sorts of gifts and coveted items but he must have his say. He cares for all comforts of his spouse and children but would like to have his spouse play the passive, submissive role. He is regular in his sexual activity and also does not make undue demands on his partner in this regard. Marriage, for him, is a saga of serious responsibility.

Life Number 2: Number 2 persons is changeable just like phases of the moon. He sometimes displays great love and affection towards his spouse and on other occasions shows an apathetic and indifferent attitude. He is, however, fully devoted to the home and domestic cause. Females of this number are adept in all their domestic chores. Even if they have to work outside, they look after all domestic needs and do full justice to their job as well as home. Males of this number often make henpecked husbands. They are particularly conscious and fussy about the food habit and nutrition of their growing children and take extra pains to ensure that they get wholesome, hygienic food. They are rather stingy in spending and tend to save for the rainy day.

Life Number 3: Number 3 person likes to interact with his spouse on equal footing. He is understanding and considerate. But he is sometimes too idealistic and unwilling to compromise on his principles. He sets serious codes for his spouse and children and expects them to follow them. Interestingly, he sets example himself by following the codes and rules. He is a practical idealist. He does not believe in undue spendings. He likes to spend liberally on his children and on family outings. Also, he is not particularly fussy about sexual matters.

Life Number 4: He generally marries late. For him married life is not a passport to sexual freedom but a serious regimen of duties and responsibilities. He likes to have many children and large families. But this can be possible only if his spouse shares his thinking in this matter. In money matters he is somewhat miserly. He likes to spend money out of real necessity rather than a need to have pomp and show or for ego satisfaction. He is either too dominating or too tolerant. He cannot be in between. His spouse should learn to live with his peculiarities and eccentricities, for, below his eccentricities is a sincere, committed and faithful self.

Life Number 5: Number 5 persons are fond of order in everything. They are finicky about details, thoroughness and systems in every activity. In married life they have a tendency to save more and spend less for they are very worrisome about the future. They are very painstaking in care of their children and in their mental and cultural upbringing. They are adjustable and adaptable to the needs of their partner in the matter of sex. However, they have a habit of criticizing everything including the nature, habits and propensities of their spouse. This tells upon marital harmony and adjustment in most cases depends on the attitude and behaviour of spouse.

Life Number 6: Males with life number 6 are fond of sensual enjoyment. This must find proper outlet. In general, number 6 persons are very particular about the interior decoration and upkeep of their homes. Things in their home and surroundings must look bright and attractive. With their cheerful disposition they maintain a lively atmosphere at home. Many No. 6 persons display youthful romance even 20 years after marriage! They spend a lot on luxuries and decorative articles. But then they also endeavour to ensure that extra income pours in their home!

Life Number 7: Number 7 persons are sometimes secretive even with their spouses. But they are very cooperative in the discharge of all household chores. Husbands of number 7 are often found helping their wives with the kitchen work! They are active and energetic in the upkeep and maintenance of house. However, they do exhibit a tendency for that extra-marital affair which they indulge in surreptitiously. In money matters, No. 7 persons are extravagant and often end up spending more than they can afford. This makes a mess of their domestic budget. Number 7 persons remain lively in the matter of sex for a long time.

Life Number 8: Number 8 persons have a serious, philosophical outlook in marital life. They are unquestionably sincere and devoted to their spouse and children. They, however, do not take much interest in the material affairs of their home. Initiatives, in this regard, have to be taken by their spouses. In the matter of sex; they are often over-indulgent. They regard sex as a physical necessity. Over-indulgence, more often than not, tells upon their health. As a rule they have few children. Number 8 persons are often rigid and stubborn in many matters which creates marital discord at times. In money matters they are very cautious and stingy but truly prudent in spending.

Life Number 9: Life number 9 persons display a tendency to dominate and force their opinion or decision on their spouse. Frank and outspoken, they are passionate love makers. They are extremely responsive to the needs of their children but are sometimes indifferent to the needs of their spouse. Females of this number often marry late while males marry early. Their children are born rather early, mostly within 3 to 4 years of marriage. Number 9 persons are also not lavish in spending. They will spend more on the needs of their children than on their homes. Short temper is an attribute of these persons which tends to undermine their conjugal harmony.

CHAPTER 16

Numbers and Famous Personalities

While providing an exposition of Numerology it is considered extremely important to present the practical illustration of the working of numbers through the lives of famous Indian and international personalities. This chapter attempts to achieve just that. A close observation of the numerological analysis of those lives would provide a remarkable testimony to the truth and accuracy of theoretical precepts given in the foregoing chapters.

In the following paragraphs is rendered numerological analysis of the lives of 20 famous personalities known in India and the world at large.

1. Mahatma Gandhi: Mahatma Gandhi, father of the Indian Nation, whose full name was Mohandas Karamchand Gandhi is a well-known figure of the 20th century India and also has international stature as a saint-reformer and a leader of the masses. Let us apply the knowledge of numbers on his life history as known to us.

Name: MOHANDAS KARAMCHAND GANDHI

Date of birth: 2-10-1869

We first determine the various numbers relating to the above individual.

Birth number : 2

Universality number (corresponding to the birth month of October): 1

Fortune number (as derived from the compound number of the year of birth): 6

Complete number (arrived at by summing up the above three numbers): 9

Ascendant number (number corresponding to the zodiac sign of the month of birth): 5

We write the above numbers again in a column form.

Various numbers as worked out
2
1
6
9
5

Examining the above array for repetition of numbers, we observe that no number repeats itself in the array. Therefore, it is only the birth number 2 which has the predominant influence over the native.

We put together now the various important events in the life of Mahatma Gandhi in chronological order.

Event	*Year*	*Corresponding simple number*
Marriage to Kasturba	1883	2
Father's demise	1885	4
Began to practice law	1892	2
Return to India from South Africa	1901	2
Quit India Movement (which was spearheaded by him)	1942	7
Assassinated	1948	4

From the above it can be easily observed that important events involving worldly success and achievement by Mahatma Gandhi occurred during years which reduce to number 2 or 7. We know that number 7 is complementary and friendly to the number 2. But at the same time, number 4 is inimical to number 2. No wonder, tragedy befell Mahatma Gandhi in years corresponding to number 4 as the above array of events illustrates.

2. Jawaharlal Nehru: He was a famous international statesman more than a freedom fighter and political leader in India. He was born on 14-11-1889.

Let us write down the various pertinent numbers.

Name	:	JAWAHARLAL NEHRU
Date of birth	:	14-11-1889
Birth number	:	5
Universality number	:	2
Fortune number	:	8
Complete number	:	6
Ascendant number	:	6

Evidently, the number 6 repeats itself and is, therefore, to be taken as the number having predominant influence on the life of Jawaharlal Nehru (or the life number, technically speaking).

Event	*Year*	*Correspond-ing simple number*
Sent to England for higher studies	1905	6
Was imprisoned while participating in freedom movement	1921	4
Became Prime Minister of free India	1947	3
Chinese aggression and losses suffered by Indian Defence Force	1962	9
Death	1964	2

Number 3 is friendly to life number 6 and is associated with favourable event. Numbers 9 and 2 are not complementary to number 6 and are associated with adverse events.

3. Indira Gandhi: Indira Gandhi was a famous political personality of modern India. Having remained in the saddle of Prime Minister of India for a period of nearly 16 years, she had contributed enormously to the development of free India, enabling it to occupy an important position on the global horizon.

We do the same exercise as before for Indira Gandhi.

Name	:	INDIRA GANDHI
Date of birth	:	19-11-1917
Birth Number	:	1

Universality number : 2
Fortune number : 9
Complete number : 3
Ascendant number : 9

Clearly, number 9 repeats itself once in the above array and is, therefore, to be taken as the life number. We now list chronologically the various important events in the life of Indira Gandhi.

Event	*Year*	*Corresponding simple number*
Father was imprisoned	1921	4
Imprisonment of self	1942	7
Birth of elder son, Rajiv	1944	9
Birth of younger son, Sanjay	1946	2
Elected chairperson of Congress Working Committee	1955	2
Death of husband Feroz Gandhi	1960	7
Elected member of Rajya Sabha (Upper House of Parliament) and subsequently made Information and Broadcasting Minister	1964	2
Expelled from Congress Working Committee	1969	7
Imposition of Emergency and led the country to victory against war with Pakistan	1971	9
Simla Agreement	1972	1
Unseated from Lok Sabha by Allahabad High Court judgement	1975	4
Again elected Prime Minister	1980	9
Assassinated	1984	4

It is again to be observed from the above that events associated with worldly success occurred in the life of Indira Gandhi during years corresponding to numbers 9, 2 and 1. The number 9 is the life number as indicated before and the numbers 1 and 2 are its friendly numbers. Further it is seen that adverse events occurred in years corresponding to number 7 which is an enemy number to the life number 9. Finally, the end of her illustrious life came in the year 1984 which corresponds to the number 4, a number inimical to life number 9.

4. Rabindranath Tagore: He was an eminent Indian of international fame. He made notable contribution to the world of literature and was awarded the much coveted Noble Prize for literature. Let us glean through his life history and apply numerological analysis to it.

Name	:	RABINDRANATH TAGORE
Date of birth	:	7th May, 1861
Birth number	:	7
Universality number	:	5
Fortune number	:	7
Complete number	:	1
Ascendant number	:	2

Clearly, number 7 repeats itself twice in the above array and is, therefore, to be regarded as life number. We now array the life events of Rabindranath Tagore chronologically.

Event	*Year*	*Corresponding simple number*
Admitted to Oriental Seminary (formal school)	1868	5
Set sail for England for higher education	1878	6
Married Mrinalini Devi	1883	2
Elected president of the Provincial Congress	1908	9
Founded the Shantiniketan School of Learning	1901	2
Lost his daughter Rani	1902	3
Lost his father	1905	6
Lost his son Samindra	1907	8
Awarded Nobel Prize for Literature for his work *Gitanjali*	1913	5
Was Knighted	1915	7
Eldest daughter Bela passed away	1918	1
Death	1941	6

In the above array of events, it is seen that all favourable events generally fall in years corresponding to number 7 or its friendly numbers (5, 9) and adverse events mostly fall in years corresponding to numbers 3, 8, 1 which are not complementary or friendly to the life number 7.

5. Annie Besant: She was famous as a humanist and a notable contributor to the building of modern India. She was also a freedom crusader and her role in the freedom struggle of India is well recognized.

Name	:	ANNIE BESANT
Date of birth	:	1st October, 1847
Birth Number	:	1
Universality number	:	1
Fortune number	:	2
Complete number	:	4
Ascendant number	:	5

Evidently, the life number of Annie Besant is 1. Putting across the various important life events of Annie Besant.

Event	*Year*	*Corresponding simple number*
Father's death	1852	7
Marriage	1867	4
Divorce	1873	1
Joined Fabian Society through association with George Bernard Shaw	1885	4
Joined Theosophical Society	1889	8
Took over leadership of Theosophical Society	1891	1
Entered the Indian political arena	1913	5
Released from internment by British Authorities in India	1917	9
Death	1933	7

Number 5 and 9 are complementary to number 1 whereas number 7 is inimical to it. This explains the turnout of favourable and unfavourable events in specific calendar years in the life of Annie Besant.

6. C.V. Raman: Chandrashekhar Venkat Raman was a celebrated Indian scientist of international fame. In a period when major scientific inventions and discoveries were confined largely to scientists and scientific institutions in Europe, Russia or America, his wonderful discoveries pushed India too on the scientific map of the world. He was rewarded with the Nobel Prize for his efforts.

Name	:	C.V. RAMAN
Date of birth	:	7th November, 1888
Birth number	:	7
Universality number	:	2
Fortune number	:	7
Complete number	:	7
Ascendant number	:	6

It is immediately evident that C. V. Raman was a very strong number 7 person. Taking 7 as the life number we write down the significant events of his life

Event	*Year*	*Correspond-ing simple number*
Stood first in the High School (Matriculation) Examination	1899	9
Published first scientific paper (in *The Philosophical Magazine*, London)	1906	7
Attached himself to the Indian Association for the Cultivation of Science, Calcutta for his scientific pursuits	1908	9
Took up the Palit chair of Physics at the above Association	1917	9
Was invited to attend the Universities Congress held at Oxford, England	1921	4
Was elected a Fellow of the Royal Society, London	1924	7
Discovered the physical phenomenon 'Raman Effect' for which Nobel Prize was awarded to him	1928	2

Appointed Director of Indian Institute of Science, Bangalore	1933	7
Death	1970	8

In the above array of events number 7 and its friendly number 9 figures against favourable and significant events in the life of C. V. Raman. Number 8, which is inimical to number 7 is associated with the most unfavourable fatality—death.

7. Lal Bahadur Shastri: He was a freedom fighter, politician and statesman. He served as the second Prime Minister of free India and like a true son of the soil achieved notable feats in leading India towards its resurgence as a socio-political entity on the world scene.

Name	:	LAL BAHADUR SHASTRI
Date of birth	:	2nd October, 1902
Birth number	:	2
Universality number	:	1
Fortune number	:	3
Complete number	:	6
Ascendant number	:	5

Since no number repeats itself we shall take the birth number 2 as the life number

Event	*Year*	*Corresponding simple number*
Joined Lala Lajpat Rai's Servants of the People Society	1926	9
Married to Lalitadevi	1928	2
Elected to UP Legislative Assembly	1937	2
Became General Secretary of the Congress Party	1951	7
Resigned as India's Railway Minister	1956	3
Elected as leader of the Congress Parliamentary Party and India's Prime Minister	1964	2
Led the country to historic triumph in war against Pakistan	1965	3
Death	1966	4

Numbers 3, 9 and 7 are complementary or friendly to the birth number 2 and hold sway over historically significant events in his life purely from the viewpoint of worldly progress. Number 4 is inimical to the birth number 2 and is, no wonder, associated with his death.

8. Dayanand Saraswati: He was one of the renaissance men of modern India. A great social reformer, his contribution towards eradication of religion bigotry and obscurantism remains unparalleled till today. Numerological analysis of his life events presents an ideal avenue for testing the veracity of the statements made hereinbefore regarding the profound influence of numbers on various facets of human life.

Name	:	DAYANAND SARASWATI
Date of birth	:	12th February, 1824
Birth number	:	3
Universality number	:	2
Fortune number	:	6
Complete number	:	2
Ascendant number	:	8

Number 2 is repetitive among the above numbers and is, therefore, the life number.

Event	*Year*	*Corresponding simple number*
Was struck by the apparent futility of idol-worship as a young boy	1838	2
Death of sister	1840	4
Left home for a life of ascetic	1846	1
Established the 'Arya Samaj'	1875	3

Among the above numbers 1, 2, 3 and 4, the numbers 1 and 3 are complementary to the life number 2 whereas the number 4 is inimical to the life number. Not surprisingly, therefore, all friendly numbers spell favourable events and inimical number otherwise.

9. Raja Ram Mohun Roy: He was a great social reformer of India of nineteenth century. His role in the awakening of the Indian society against the evils of the prevailing superstitious and other social practices is perhaps equalled by none.

Name	:	RAJA RAM MOHUN ROY
Date of birth	:	22nd May, 1772
Birth number	:	4
Universality number	:	5
Fortune number	:	8
Complete number	:	8
Ascendant number	:	6

Number 8 presents itself twice in the above computation and, accordingly, plays the role of life number.

Event	*Year*	*Correspond-ing simple number*
Joined the Civil Service of the British East India Company.	1805	5
Set up the 'Atmiya Sabha' (House of retrospection or soul searching)	1815	6
Started Anglo-Hindu School	1822	4
Founded the Brahmo Samaj (Society for the Followers of the Absolute) which was a cause of immediate popular revulsion and rebuke against him	1828	1

It is again observed events connected with material success and happiness are associated with friendly numbers 4, 5 and 6 and event connected with opposite type of aspects is associated with the number 1 which is inimical to the life number 8.

10. Srinivas Ramanujam: Srinivas Ramanujam was a greater scholar and researcher of mathematics who achieved international fame for his brilliant discoveries. His contribution to the field of mathematics shall always be remembered by the posterity.

Name : SRINIWAS RAMANUJAM
Date of birth : 22nd December, 1887
Birth number : 4
Universality number : 3
Fortune number : 6
Complete number : 4
Ascendant number : 3

In this array both 4 and 3 repeat themselves once. But 4, being the birth number, is to be taken as the life number.

Event	*Year*	*Corresponding simple number*
Secured admission in an England's University for pursuing higher education in Mathematics	1913	5
Elected Fellow of the Royal Society	1918	1
Death	1920	3

The life number is 4; 1 and 5 are its friendly numbers and 3 is its inimical number. The influence of these numbers on the life events of Ramanujam is indicated by the above account of events.

11. Jayaprakash Narayan: Jayaprakash Narayan is famous as a socio-political revolutionary of modern India. Cast in the Gandhian mould, he is credited for having shaped the thinking and attitudes of millions of Indians in the direction of cleaning public life of crime and corruption. His contribution towards social and political reform in the post independence period is, perhaps, second to none.

Name : JAYAPRAKASH NARAYAN
Date of birth : 11th October, 1902
Birth number : 2
Universality number : 1
Fortune number : 3
Complete number : 6
Ascendant number : 5

Here again, we take the birth number 2 as life number because no number repeats itself.

Event	*Year*	*Corresponding simple number*
Married Prabhavati	1920	3
Set sail for America for the purpose of higher education	1922	5
Jailed for participating in Civil Disobedience Movement	1930	4
Released from jail	1933	7
Arrested for opposing India's participation in the Second World War on behalf of the British	1940	5
Imprisoned again after escape from jail and sent to Lahore Fort torture chamber	1943	8
Released finally from jail	1946	2
Announced dedication of his life to Sarvodaya Movement	1954	1
Organised Janata Party as an alternative to ruling Congress Party	1977	6
Death	1979	7

Unfavourable events from the worldly viewpoint clearly fall in years with numbers 4 and 8 which are inimical to birth number and life number 2. Favourable events correspond to numbers 1, 3 and 5.

Number 7 is considered neutral to number 2. Death in the case of Jayaprakash Narayan cannot be considered unfavourable because he died a contented man, having achieved what he had set out as his life objectives.

12. Dr. S. Radhakrishnan: Eminent educationist, philosopher and statesman—Dr. Radhakrishnan was all in one. From a teacher he rose to the position of President of Indian Republic.

Name : SARVAPALLI RADHAKRISHNAN
Date of birth 5th September, 1888

Birth number : 5
Universality number : 9
Fortune number : 7
Complete number : 3
Ascendant number : 1

Here again, we take 5 as the life number, since no number repeats itself.

Event	*Year*	*Corresponding simple number*
Got married	1904	5
Took up teaching job at Madras Presidency College	1909	1
Selected as Professor of Philosophy by the University of Mysore	1918	1
Published his famous work, *Indian Philosophy*	1923	6
Became Vice-Chancellor of the Andhra University	1931	5
Selected as chairman of University Education Commission	1948	4
Chosen India's first envoy to Soviet Union	1949	5
Death of wife	1956	3
Elected second President of the Republic of India	1962	9
Death	1975	4

Analysing the above events in a generalised perspective, it is seen that events which are extremely significant occurred in years corresponding to number 5, which is the same as life number! This again testifies to the remarkable accuracy of the specific influence of numbers in shaping the lives of humans and in precipitating their life events. In the above statement of events, the only unfavourable event mentioned was the death of his wife which took place in 1956, corresponding to simple number 3. Number 3 is inimical to the birth number/life number 5.

13. Sir Isaac Newton: He is regarded as one of the greatest scientific geniuses in the history of mankind.

To this seventeenth century scientist, we owe a great number of original scientific discoveries and inventions which formed the basis of the industrial and technological revolution of the following three hundred years—revolution which has virtually changed the face of the globe.

Name	:	Isaac Newton
Date of birth	:	25th December, 1642
Birth number	:	7
Universality number	:	3
Fortune number	:	4
Complete number	:	5
Ascendant number	:	8

Since no number is repetitive, we have to regard the birth number 7 as the life number.

Event	*Year*	*Correspond-ing simple number*
Graduated from Trinity College	1665	9
Discovered the Binomial Theorem	1665	9
Selected to a Fellowship of Trinity	1667	2
Invented the Reflecting Telescope	1668	3
Serious illness	1727	8
Death (on March 20)	1727	8

To the number 7, friendly/complementary numbers are 1, 2 and 9; the number 3 is neutral to it and numbers 4, 8 and 6 can be regarded as uncomplimentary. Events of significance in the life of Sir Isaac Newton which gave him worldly success and recognition of efforts are clearly, associated with the complementary numbers 2 and 9. The number 8 brought him serious illness and death, again testifying to the truth of the philosophy of numbers mentioned in this work.

14. Abraham Lincoln: He was one of those rare earthy men who rise from petty and humble position to the pinnacles of power and authority. From the position of a clerk in a general store in Illinois, he went on to become the President of the United States of America. His role as a great statesman and leader of the masses is recognised to this day.

Name	:	ABRAHAM LINCOLN
Date of birth	:	12th February, 1809
Birth number	:	3
Universality number	:	2
Fortune number	:	9
Complete number	:	5
Ascendant number	:	4

In this case also, we take the birth number as the life number because no number is repetitive. Regarding 3 as the life number,

Event	*Year*	*Corresponding simple number*
Led into farm work (which he enjoyed exceedingly)	1830	3
Contested for the Legislature but lost	1832	5
Elected to the Lower House of Congress	1846	1
Assassination	1865	2

Here also we observe that years corresponding to numbers 1 and 3 are favourable to the native and the year corresponding to number 5 is unfavourable. The numbers 1 and 3 are friendly to the birth number 3 and number 5 is inimical to the birth number. In the case of assassination of Abraham Lincoln, we again observe the anomaly, i.e., the number associated with the year of assassination is 2 which is complementary to life number 3. The explanation to this is that Abraham Lincoln had achieved some kind of philosophical satisfaction from life and himself did not value his life much. He was more than prepared to sacrifice his life for his avowed objectives – removal of slavery and discrimination and establishment of democracy. As such we do not see in his assassination an event which he shuddered or wished to avoid as most ordinary mortals do.

15. Michelangelo Buonarroti: Michelangelo was a painter and sculptor of the sixteenth century Europe whose distinguished pieces of work have left an indelible mark on the posterity. His genius is recognised even after four centuries of his death and he remains a model of inspiration for the artist of today.

Name	:	MICHELANGELO BUONARROTI
Date of birth	:	6th March, 1475
Birth number	:	6
Universality number	:	3
Fortune number	:	8
Complete number	:	8
Ascendant number	:	3

Here, we have a piquant situation. In the above array of numbers, 3 and 8 both repeat themselves once. But of these two numbers, it is the number 8 which is to be given the greater significance as it is friendly to the birth number 6. As such the number 8 is to be regarded as the life number of Michelangelo.

Event	*Year*	*Corresponding simple number*
Began his first work of sculpture (Statue of David)	1502	8
Began work on the tomb of Julius II (took up work rather hesitantly, in adverse circumstances)	1522	1
Finished work on tomb of Julius II	1545	6
Death	1564	7

By and large, a similar association of numbers and events can be observed in the life of Michelangelo as illustrated in the lives of famous persons of history earlier in this chapter.

16. Adolf Hitler: Adolf Hitler is famous as the German dictator who held powerful sway over Nazis and incorporated military attitudes and techniques into politics. He is considered as a person responsible for precipitating the Second World War which left a trail of terrible death and destruction. Let us see how numbers explain the life events of Adolf Hitler.

Name	:	ADOLF HITLER
Date of birth	:	20th April, 1889
Birth number	:	2
Universality number	:	4
Fortune number	:	8
Complete number	:	5
Ascendant number	:	2

From the above it is at once clear that the life number of Adolf Hitler is 2. Putting down the important events in his life, we write as below.

Event	*Year*	*Correspond-ing simple number*
Death of father	1903	4
Death of mother	1907	8
Joined the German Workers' Party	1919	2
Attempted to seize power in the State of Bavaria (but failed)	1923	6
Won majority (288 seats) in German Parliamentary Elections	1933	7
Defeat of Germany in the battle of Stalingrad (under the leadership of Hitler)	1943	8
Committed suicide	1945	1

In all the above events we once again observe the association of favourable events with numbers friendly to life number.

The only apparent exception is the last event of Hitler's death. When we analyse the circumstances in which he committed suicide, we realize that death was indeed a saving grace for him for, if alive, he would have been subjected to the worst torture by his enemies. Viewed in that light, Hitler saved himself from bitter dishonour, torture and subjugation—conditions which for him were worse than death.

In Hitler's life, events in the years 1919 and 1933 both associated with rise in political career and success correspond to numbers which are friendly to the life number 2.

17. Mao Tse-Tung: Mao was regarded as the father of communism and modern utopia in China. A great leader of the masses, he has left an indelible impression on the lives of millions of people of China. His philosophies and style of leadership were able to instil nationalism, patriotism and progressive attitudes in the Chinese. His life events are outlined below.

Name	:	MAO TSE-TUNG
Date of birth	:	26th December, 1893
Birth number	:	8
Universality number	:	3
Fortune number	:	3
Complete number	:	5
Ascendant number	:	8

Here, again numbers 8 as well as 3 repeat themselves. But since number 8 is birth number, we regard it as the life number also.

Event	*Year*	*Corresponding simple number*
Uprising began against Mao's Communist Party; Mao was arrested and sentenced to death	1927	1
Defeated his political adversary Chiang Kai-Shek	1930	4
Mao's Communist Party grew in size and stature after he successfully accomplished a political campaign and propaganda plan	1934	8
Chinese Civil War erupts	1945	1
Mao's Communist Party emerged victorious in Chinese Civil War	1949	5
Began the Great-Leap Forward in China—an economic drive of great historical significance	1958	5
Death	1976	5

Number 5 is friendly/neutral to the birth number 8; number 1 is inimical to the birth number 8 and number 4 is complementary to it. Chairman Mao had a long, contented and successful life. He died a satisfied man whose personal ideas and principles which found expression in his leadership style succeeded remarkably in giving China the high status that it enjoys among the comity of nations today.

18. John F. Kennedy: The famous president of the United States was a true champion of human rights. He worked earnestly for assuaging global tension caused by threat of war. His bold approach in counteracting Russian military designs in Cuba earned him applause. He would for long be remembered as a great leader wedded to the ideals of true freedom, equality and international peace.

Name	:	JOHN F. KENNEDY
Date of birth	:	29th May, 1917
Birth number	:	2
Universality number	:	5
Fortune number	:	9
Complete number	:	7
Ascendant number	:	5

Clearly, the life number is 5.

Event	*Year*	*Corresponding simple number*
Became a United States Senator from Massachusetts	1952	8
Contested for Vice-Presidency of US but was unsuccessful	1956	3
Returned to Senate with a resounding majority	1958	5
Elected US President	1960	7
Assassinated	1963	1

John Kennedy was assassinated in the year 1963 corresponding to the number 1. Now the number 1 again is not unfriendly to the life number 5. What does it mean? A successful and well spent life, even if drastically cut short, may not always be taken to mean a tragic event from the point of view of the individual in question.

19. George Washington: He was an illustrious political head and a great man. He is credited with the rise of the American nation and its elevation to the level of its present glory. His excellent statesmanship and exquisite political leadership have left deep impression on world history, an impression that time will not be able to fade.

Name	:	GEORGE WASHINGTON
Date of birth	:	22nd February, 1732
Birth number	:	4
Universality number	:	2
Fortune number	:	4
Complete number	:	1
Ascendant number	:	8

Here, 4 which is repetitive and being the birth number is to be regarded as the life number. We now chart out the important events in the illustrious life of George Washington.

Event	*Year*	*Corresponding simple number*
Marriage to Martha Custis	1759	4
Was made the General Commanding by the Continental Congress	1775	2
Achieved Army Victory at Brandyarne and Germantown	1777	4
Elected President of the United States of America	1789	7
Death	1799	8

From the above array of events it is gleaned that George Washington's life illustrates the working of numbers like that of any other person. Although he died at a relatively younger age, he had achieved the goals he had personally set in his life.

20. Louis XVI: He was the famous king of France during the time of the French revolution. His deft handling of the French nation during the turbulent years of the revolution through excellent administrative abilities and stewardship of a high order has left an deep mark on the pages of world history.

Name	:	LOUIS XVI
Date of birth	:	23rd August, 1754
Birth number	:	5
Universality number	:	8
Fortune number	:	8
Complete number	:	3
Ascendant number	:	1

From the above it is obvious that the ruling life number applicable to Louis XVI is 8. A look into his life events would highlight the working of this number in the life of King Louis XVI

Event	*Year*	*Corresponding simple number*
Death of father	1765	1
Marriage to Marie Antoinette, the Empress of Austria	1770	6
Coronation in Rheims Cathedral	1775	2
King Louis Swore to maintain the constitution at the Festival of the Federation (a historical event)	1790	8
Death of trusted confidant and deputy of the National Assembly Mirabean	1791	9
Brought to trial on the charge of treason	1793	2
Death on the scaffold	1793	2

The influence of the life number 8 in shaping important events in the life of King Louis XVI is markedly brought out above. We can observe that favourable events in the life of Louis XVI are associated with numbers 6 and 8 which are in harmony with the life number 8 whereas unfavourable events are associated with the numbers 1 and 2 which are in disharmony with the life number.

CHAPTER 17

Numerology and Important Events

Numbers have a vast purview of action and influence. As already discussed before, numbers appear to control the lives of human beings. The previous chapters have attempted to provide the theoretical precepts and the practical working of numbers in shaping the life and destiny of human beings. But numbers hold an equally important sway over the working of human institutions, mundane events and also events of geographical and astronomical significance. It would be interesting to see the working of numbers in some of the well-known events in the history of the world.

1. The Year 1666: The Great Fire of London—The number 1666 reduces to the simple number 1 which stands for Sun. Sun rules fires and all phenomena connected with fire. The Great Fire of London which occurred in the year 1666 is famous to this day after 331 years as one of the greatest fire accidents in world history.

2. The Year 1707: Act of Union between England and Scotland —During the sixteenth and seventeenth centuries, Britain was the major world power and its empire extended over a large number of countries across the continents of the globe. The unification of England and Scotland is an event of great historical significance. Interestingly, it occurred in the calendar year 1707 which numerically reduces to the number 6. The curious reader may refer to the significations of number 6 which stands for associations, alliances, unifications and friendships.

3. The Year 1789: French Revolution begins—If we add up the numbers 1, 7, 8 and 9 constituting the year 1789, we obtain the total 25 which when simplified yields the number 7. This number stands for the lunar node 'Ketu' which is associated with revolutionary changes. The French Revolution is a significant event in the history of Europe which led to the enactment of new constitution in France and declaration of the French republic. This had important repercussions for the subsequent socio-political life in the whole of Europe.

4. The Year 1831: Dynamo and Transformer invented by Michael Faraday—Adding up the numbers 1, 8, 3 and 1 gives the number 13 which is equivalent to the simple number of 4. This takes us back to the description of the number 4 provided earlier in this book. This number symbolises 'Rahu', the shadowy planet. Rahu governs electricity and all electrical machinery. It is, therefore, not a coincidence that electric dynamo and transformer were invented in a calendar year ruled by 'Rahu'! And undoubtedly the invention of these items formed the very foundation of electrical power industry in the years to follow.

5. The Year 1903: First aeroplane flight by Wilbur and Orville Wright (US)—The invention of aeroplane is a great landmark in modern world history. This event has revolutionised global life by bridging the barriers of time and geographical boundary in international dealings. The year 1903 reduces to the simple number 4, which is ruled by Uranus as per Western Astrology and by the shadowy planet 'Rahu' as per Classical Hindu Astrology. Both planets govern scientific research. The invention of aeroplane has been a great leap for mankind in the field of science.

6. The Year 1931: Telex machine was invented. Telex machine for the purpose of rapid transmission of messages was invented in the year 1931. This number totals up to 14 and reduces to the simple number of 5 which governs communications of all sorts. It is no wonder that this great invention which revolutionised communication occurred in the calendar year corresponding to number 5, the number of communications!

7. The Year 1957: Russians launched Sputnik I, the first artificial earth satellite. The space age really began in 1957 with the launching of Russian satellite Sputnik I. This was followed by the

USA launching Explorer I and the two superpowers engaged in a space race. By the year 1986, the spacecraft Voyager 2 was sending pictures of the planet Uranus to earth. In the subject of space exploration the year 1957 is significant because the first exploratory spacecraft was set off in this year. Total up the numbers 1, 9, 5 and 7 and you get 22. Add up 2 and 2 and you get 4, the number of revolutionary discoveries and exploration.

8. The Year 1969: Man lands on the moon. On the historical day of 20th April, 1969, American astronauts (of the spaceship Apollo 11) Neil Armstrong and Edwin Aldrin landed on the moon. Interestingly, 1969 simplifies to the number 7 which, ruled by Neptune, signifies aviation and space. Another interesting point to note in this regard is that the actual date of this landmark event, i.e., 20th April is reducible to number 2 which is ruled by none other than the planet Moon!

9. The Year 1989: Communist rule ends in East Germany and the Berlin Wall dividing East and West Germany is demolished. The year 1989 is also famous for the end of Communist rule in Bulgaria, Czechoslovakia, Hungary and Romania. End of Communism in all these countries is considered as a historical event of global ramifications and significance.

Just add up the numbers 1, 9, 8 and 9. What do you get? The sum obtained is 27 which reduces to number 9. The number 9 is ruled by Mars which signifies freedom and rebelliious independence in contrast to number 8 (ruled by Saturn) which is the number of communism.

10. The Year 1992: Democrat William Bill Clinton defeats Republican George Bush in US Presidential election. Yugoslavia breaks up as Bosnia/Herzegovina and Macedonia declares independence. The year 1992 can be considered as the year of self-determination and the triumph of democracy. Let us see how. Adding up the numbers 1, 9, 9 and 2 yields 21 which reduces to the number 3. The number 3 signifies independence and end of oppression. It also signifies democracy.

In the above paragraphs the working of simple numbers in influencing world events has been illustrated. World events in specific terms are determined and shaped by a multitude of factors like the country in which the event occurred, its social, political and cultural scenario, geographical factors, etc. As far as numerological analysis of any such world event is concerned, it is really not a simple and straightforward affair. The fundamental approach of numerological analysis for human individuals which comprises determination of birth number, universality number, fortune number, etc., is analogously applicable to formal institutions and nations also. Therefore, merely knowledge of the simple number derived from the compound number corresponding to event-year cannot suffice for analysis of every world event. However in the foregoing pages were analysed events not of national but of global significance. These are some of the events which have dramatically altered the historical course of the global community directly or indirectly. And the simplified year number is the most powerful, determinant of these events.

CHAPTER 18

Numbers in Health and Disease

In Chapter 4 giving a detailed exposition of the numbers 1 to 9, some account was provided of the types of diseases that persons having life numbers 1 to 9 are prone to and the suggestive remedial measures in terms of food habits and general lifestyle. It appears strange but it is amazingly true that a person is susceptible to typical diseases according to his life number. This chapter endeavours to present in broader detail the role of specific numbers in health and disease with a special emphasis on proper prevention and treatment. While on the subject of health and medicine, it would also be appropriate to clarify that specific numbers also govern specific schools of medicine and surgery. They also symbolise various different types of drugs. Therefore, in the numerological context, it is easy as well as prudent to apply the significations of numbers for preparing profiles of health and medical advice for persons in accordance with their life numbers.

Number 1 persons (persons with life number 1) have a tendency to suffer from ailments connected with excess of heat in their body. They often suffer from obesity, excess of cholesterol, heart disease, troubles with the eyesight, formation of stones in the gall bladder, sunstrokes, biliousness, hepatitis, engorgement of the liver. What is their prescription for good health?

To keep the excess of biliousness and body heat in control, they should avoid the intake of fatty and oily foodstuffs. Red meat is perhaps the worst poison for them. Among vegetable, tomato, turnip and brinjal are to be avoided. The kind of foodstuffs that will do much good to them are rice, barley, milk, curd and yoghurt, cabbage, radish, cucumber, gourd. They should drink as much water as possible. Egg is another food item which is prescribed for them. Herbal medicines are very effective for their ailments. In cases of marked structural changes caused by diseases, surgical intervention is also useful.

The periods of the calendar year in which number 1 persons are most susceptible to ill-health are 13th May to 14th June, 17th October to 13th November, 14th January to 13th February and 14th February to 13th March.

Number 2 persons (those having life number 2) are vulnerable to such ailments as catarrh, colds and influenza, gastritis, diarrhoea, conjunctivitis, glaucoma, mastitis, breast cancer, boils and carbuncles, anaemia, pharyngitis, tonsillitis, typhoid, cholera, chickenpox, smallpox, mumps, measles, meningitis, pneumonia, insomnia.

Most of the above diseases are either due to excess of phlegm in the body or because of defective water metabolism. The dietary prescription for number 2 persons is that they should restrict the intake of phlegm forming foods like rice, curds, milk, beetroot. They should also avoid excess of sleep and should be particularly careful not to sleep during daytime unless severely fatigued. They should take regular exercise and not slip into a sedentary lifestyle. Among vegetables raw onion is not suitable for their constitution and should be avoided. Citrus fruits are good and should be taken in moderate quantities. Raw salad vegetables good for them are carrot, tomatoes,turnip and garlic. Finally, they should be extracareful about cleanliness and hygiene. Number 2 persons benefit a lot from treatment by the modern allopathic drugs because they tend to suffer from frequent infections. They also benefit from surgery. The periods in the year in which ill-health can strike number 2 persons are 13th May to 14th June, 17th October to 13th November, 14th January to 13th February and 13th April to 12th March.

This takes us to number 3 persons. Number 3 is ruled by Jupiter and this planet rules liver functions and regulates fat metabolism in the human body. Number 3 persons are predisposed to all liver diseases like jaundice, chronic hepatitis and cirrhosis.They are also prone to obesity and various types of visceral inflammations. Many diseases that afflict number 3 persons result from excesses of various types. Overindulgence in rich food, sex, liquor or even excessive exercise are the causes of these diseases. These diseases include dyspepsia, disorders of the lymphatic system, overactivity of endocrine glands like pituitary, thyroid and hypothalamus and enlargement of the heart or spleen. Hypertension is another common ailment that troubles number 3 persons. Other ailments afflicting number 3 persons are backache, spondylitis, rheumatism, appendicitis and oedema.

The answer to all the above health problems lies in moderation in habits and a regulated life-style. Avoidance of rich, spicy and fast serving food is their recipe for good health. Any kind of extra strain on mind, nervous system or rest of the body is bound to have deleterious effects on health. So the best course of action for these people is to ensure adequate rest of the mind as well as the body.

Most of the drugs and courses of treatment available under Allopathic system can only serve to palliate the symptoms of diseases suffered by number 3 persons. They can better benefit from the Ayurvedic system of medicine or even from Naturopathic techniques of treatment.

From the viewpoint of zodiac signs, the following periods of the year could be the most difficult for number 3 persons 13th May to 14th June, 15th June to 15th July, 17th September to 16th October and 17th October to 13th November.

Number 4 persons tend to suffer from rheumatism, skin ailments, bronchitis, allergic conditions of the nose and throat, chronic catarrhs, constipation, stomach and duodenum ulcers, mental illnesses, mania, melancholia. Many of their diseases remain undetected. They often suffer from mysterious ailments which are difficult to diagnose and treat. This is because of the natural influence of the ruling planet 'Rahu'. Number 4 persons frequently suffer from psychosomatic illnesses which result purely from emotional disturbances.

Number 4 persons are advised to avoid drugs of all kinds. They should undertake Naturopathic treatment for their ailments. They also benefit immensely from auto suggestion in cases of mental illness. Number 4 persons sometimes form a major portion of the patient lists of psychiatrists and psychotherapists. But they, more often than not, benefit maximum from self-education and auto-suggestion in all these cases.

Number 4 persons are advised to eschew rich and highly seasoned food and keep their diet as bland as possible. They should particularly avoid eggs and meat. Many number 4 persons are near gluttons because of a voracious appetite. But they should be choosy about their diet if not moderate in eating.

The periods of the calendar year in which to take better care of their health are given below:

April 13th to 12th May, 16th July to 16th August, 17th August to 16th September, 14th November to 14th December.

We now come over to the life number 5. Persons having 5 as their life number are prone to nervous ailments, diseases of the intestines, oral cavity, nose, throat and ear. Some of the typical diseases to which thesc people are susceptible are nervous debility, neuritis, epilepsy, dysentery, chronic diarrhoea, chronic otorrhoea, rhinitis, sinusitis, eczema, dermatitis, nasal polyps.

For number 5 persons, the best advice is to keep mental tension at bay and prevent overstraining of the nervous system. Many of these persons have a tendency to worry too much which fritters away their nervous energy. If they learn to develop a calm and quiet disposition, they would do much good to their health. In the matter of diet, they are advised to take a balanced diet and not to be finicky about what to eat. They should freely take all types of foods in moderate quantities, not allowing their appetite to be spoilt by worry and emotional stress. The following calendar periods are adverse for their health and call for greater care.

13th April to 12th May, 15th December to 13th January and 14th March to 12th April.

Number 6 persons are ruled by Venus and are usually endowed with sound physique and robust constitution. They generally remain healthy and disease-free unless they indulge in serious indiscretions of diet, sex, sleep or even exercise. Many number 6 persons have an obsession for fitness and beauty and in the process tend to overdo beauty treatments and physical exercises. This becomes prejudicial to their health and often drains their vitality and energy.

Various diseases that tend to afflict number 6 persons include urinary and bladder infection, prostatitis, sexual inadequacies and diseases of sex organs, sterility, sexually transmitted diseases, diabetes, uterine disorders, leucorrhoea, cough, cold and catarrh, nervous debility.

Regarding medico-numerological advice for number 6 persons, they should try to observe moderation in various activities and not give in to excesses. Thus avoiding violation of the laws of nature is their best bet for maintaining good health. When they are afflicted with serious diseases, allopathic treatment works best on them. They should be particularly careful to avoid becoming promiscuous and, as far as possible, maintain single sex partner.

The periods in the year which are adverse for them from health point of view are—16th July to 16 August, 17th August to 16th September and 15th December to 13th January.

Number 7 persons are prone to suffer from complicated skin diseases like psoriasis, skin cancer, ringworm, chronic fungal infections, carbuncles and athlete's foot. They are also susceptible to such ailments like chronic headaches, ulcers, fistulas and even leprosy. Besides, they sometimes tend to suffer from nervous diseases like stammering and stuttering, neuralgia, etc. Many number 7 persons are liable to contract sexually transmitted diseases. Typhoid, measles, asthma, palpitation and pericarditis are some of the other diseases which afflict them.

Number 7 persons benefit more from Herbal and Ayurvedic medical formulations than the Allopathic drugs. Often structural changes in the body caused by long standing diseases are well tackled by surgery. But purely from the numerological point of view, it is the herbal medicines which are most beneficial and efficacious for number 7 persons.

Many number 7 persons are chain-smokers and many other inveterate alcoholics. Some persons are even found to be fond of tobacco, marijuana or other depressant drugs. Once into the habit of these narcotic drugs, it becomes difficult to get out of it. Herbal therapy and Yoga are some of the effective means to help them get over the habit of drugs. In any case the best advice for them is not to succumb to the habitual desire of intoxicants in the first stage.

Number 7 persons are also in the habit of overworking their nervous system. If they take sufficient sleep, it is fine but if they curtail their sleep they invite health problems for themselves. Early to bed and early to rise is the best advice for these persons in this regard. They should try to avoid highly fatty foods and fried dishes. Also dry fruits like cashews, almonds and raisins would cause troubles to them. The intake of these items should be from little to moderate. Radish, onion, milk and rice, are excellent food items for these persons and will do good to their health.

The following periods in the year are not conducive to good health for number 7 persons :

15th June to 15th July, 17th September to 16th October, 14th January to 13th February and 14th February to 13th March.

Number 8 persons are ruled by Saturn. Saturn is the planet of obstruction, retardation, decay and degeneration. Diseases afflicting number 8 persons are connected with all these phenomena. Constipation, piles, gout, arthritis, dental decay, tuberculosis, low blood pressure, severe anaemia, spondylitis, physical and mental retardation, diseases of the circulatory system like thickening of the arteries and clot formation therein, pleurisy, lung cancer, cancer of the liver and colon, asthma, slowing down of the endocrine functions, etc.

Saturnine ailments respond well to allopathic drugs. Therefore, number 8 persons should undertake allopathic treatment as a prudent choice. They must take a balanced diet full of fresh fruits and raw vegetables and try to keep tension away. They should be particularly careful to observe moderation in sexual activity. Hyperactive sex life invites troubles for them. They should avoid late night dinners and get to sleep early at the proper time at night. Keeping awake till late night is the worst thing they can do for their health. Constipation, piles and anal fistula are extremely common diseases afflicting number 8 persons. These can be avoided simply by finishing off the evening meals within one hour after sunset. Number 8 persons should also avoid hard, strenuous exercise.

Number 9 persons are ruled by Mars and their typical diseases include fevers—both acute and chronic, inflammatory conditions of body organs in general, hypertension, toxaemia, boils, measles, haemorrhage, mumps, tumours, miscarriage and abortion, haemophilia, acute headaches.

The bad effects of the ruling planet can be avoided by preventing conditions which result in inflammatory states of the body as well as physical and mental stress. Stress is likely to be more harmful for number 9 persons than to other classes. High degree of emotional stress can precipitate strokes manifesting in conditions as serious as heart attacks and brain haemorrhage. In fact haemorrhage anywhere in the body is an extremely serious condition and needs utmost and urgent medical attention. Number 9 persons often undergo surgeries which correct their conditions. However, for most of the relatively minor ailments, they would benefit most from herbal as well as naturopathic treatments. Number 9 persons should avoid the use of highly spicy and deep fried foods. They should take plenty of green vegetables like beans, lady's finger, gourd, radish. Mint is one herb which is excellent for their constitution. It cools down their overheated, often overworked system. Periods of the calendar year which pose health problems to number 9 persons are:

15th June to 15th July, 14th January to 13th February and 12th February to 13th March.

CHAPTER 19

Numbers and Human Names

The formal or popular names of persons can be translated into numbers and these compound numbers can be reduced to simple numbers. A striking similarity is then observed between the significations of these simple numbers and the characteristics of the persons. This amazing correspondence can be best illustrated by practical examples of well-known personalitics. We shall, for the sake of simplicity take up the cases of some of the personalities of chapter 13.

1. MAHATMA GANDHI

MAHATMA	GANDHI
4 1 5 1 4 4 1	3 1 5 4 5 1
20	19
2	1

Adding 2 and 1 gives 3. Mahatma Gandhi's personality closely corresponds to many significations of number 3 given in Chapter 4. Some of these are qualities as physical and mental discipline, steadfastness and determination. Mahatma Gandhi was a truly practicalist—philosopher, a firm believer in God and religion and a committed philanthropist. All these attributes belong to number 3 subjects as described in Chapter 4.

2. JAWAHARLAL NEHRU

JAWAHARLAL	NEHRU
1 1 6 1 5 1 2 3 1 3	5 5 5 2 6
24	23
6	5

6 and 5 add up to 11 which is equivalent to the simple number 2. Prominent attributes of a number 2 ruled person are—A highly

emotional nature, very sensitive, gifted with a sound imaginative power that gives excellent artistic talent. Further, number 2 persons are distinctly peace-loving and hate to indulge in violence. Jawaharlal Nehru had all these attributes. His initiatives for promoting international peace are well known. The description of number 2 person rendered under Chapter 4 further states—'The emotional and artistic bent of mind in you creates profound interest in arts, literature and music.' We all know of Nehru's profound interest in literature and the world famous books that he has authored.

3.	INDIRA	GANDHI
	154121	3 1 5 4 5 1
	14	19
	5	1

5 and 1 add up to 6. The name Indira Gandhi, therefore, is numerologically equivalent to number 6. Reproducing the characteristics of number 6 persons given before, your life has special place for all these aspects (beauty, arts and diplomacy, love and affection, comforts and conveyances) if you are a number 6 person. You are active, energetic and have a lot of self-esteem as well as self-confidence.' Indira Gandhi as a personality epitomises all these qualities. Further it is written "You dress up well and are fond of latest fashions in clothes, shoes, even latest hair-styles!" Indira Gandhi's living habits exemplified it.

4.	DAYANAND	SARASWATI
	4 1 1 1 5 1 5 4	3 1 2 1 3 6 1 4 1
	22	22
	4	4

The name number of Dayanand Saraswati works out to 8. As per the description of number 8 persons given under Chapter 4, the personal life of Dayanand Saraswati, showed that, indeed, he was serious, patient, contented, charitable and industrious. He had that never-say-die attitude in all his tasks and missions. He had exceptional qualities of perseverance and a remarkable revolutionary spirit. That his actions were effective and productive was amply proved by the fact that he succeeded considerably in stemming the rot of obscurantism and religious bigotry in one of the most turbulent periods of modern history in India.

5. ISAAC NEWTON
   13113 556475
   9 32
   9 5

The name number of Isaac Newton is 9+5 = 14 or 5.

Referring back again to the description of number 5 persons, these persons are learned, intelligent, fast friends, benevolent and quick-thinking. They are adjustable and flexible by nature. Their sharp minds are capable of thinking and analysing rapidly. Isaac Newton possessed all these qualities.

Number 5, ruled by Mercury represents intellect and genius. It was Newton's intellectual sharpness and genius that enabled him to make such remarkable discoveries in the fields of science and mathematics.

6. ADOLF HITLER
   14738 514352
   23 20
   5 2

In case of Adolf Hitler, the famous German dictator, the name number is 5+2 = 7. Let us rewrite some typical attributes of number 7 persons.

- highly ambitious and imaginative by nature, also progressive and hardworking.
- originality, creativity and frankness are the special features of their character. They are frank even to the extent of being straightforward and outspoken.
- basically adventurous by nature.
- possess high degree of excitability and irritability.
- they are inclined to undertake big things, megaprojects and big, innovative schemes. It would be no exaggeration to say that Adolf Hitler's personality clearly exhibited all the above characteristics.

At this juncture, it is considered desirable to draw the subtle distinction between life number and name number. Whereas the life number has a very broad purview of influence, the name number is far more specific. Thus, the characteristics of an individual are better described by name number. However, there is, as we have seen above, no inconsistency between the significations of the life number and the name number, testifying to the wonderful accuracy of the principles of numerology.

The Magic of Numbers: An Overview

Numbers have intrigued scientists and philosophers for a long time. The remarkable periodicity of numbers in the phenomena of nature, the association of specific numbers with key events in the lives of human beings and also the extensive application range of numbers in formulation and implementation of scientific theories is amazing.

Numerology as a science of numbers is really a vast subject of study and practice. Its purview extends from mere mathematical laws to practically all spheres of learning. The occult significance of numbers and numerology as an occult science is but one dimension of the vast science of numbers. While bringing this little exposition of numerology to an end, it would be worthwhile to throw some light on the practical application of numerology purely from the standpoint of beneficial intervention in human problems.

Many a case has come to light wherein change in one particular alphabet in a person's name has provided a significant change in direction of life and increased good fortune. It has also enabled successful resolution of vexing problems afflicting a person. Change of name number, therefore, is acknowledged as a viable interventional tool for handling a wide range of human problems. Similarly, change in the name of the city, house or street of residence has, on many occasions, triggered a series of cataclysmic changes which have dramatically altered the fortunes of people.

Application of the principles of numerology explained in this book in our daily life, however, calls for a little bit of analysis as well as caution. This is because of the fact that cultural factors of the global civilization are dynamic or continuously changing. What is beneficial today may be regarded as baneful tomorrow. The rapid progress of science and technology has resulted in tremendous changes in perceptions, definitions and values of various life aspects. Therefore, every human being must see what is good for him having regard to his specific needs, his socio-cultural environment, his own abilities and the resources at his command. Self-analysis and introspection would be extremely useful exercises for arriving at concrete bases upon which the edifice of successful numerological application can be built.

Occult science is like an ocean consisting of many known and practised fields of study like Astrology, Palmistry, Graphology and Numerology. A learned Occult Scientist who has perfected himself in the art of prediction can be expected to give accurate prediction of future events through any one of these known branches of Occult Science. But, in practice, the common student and practitioner of Occult Science is far from ideal. He has to lean on a knowledge of all these branches to be able to crystalise his prediction. The róle of intuition is also very important in this context. Intuition or 'sixth sense' is a faculty which develops through spiritual training. A person with a well-developed intuition can gaze into the future as if seeing a mirror. However, for the vast majority of ordinary mortals, the Science of Numerology based on ancient aphorisms and empirically proven through observation and experience is certainly an effective tool for seeing through the natures of people, worldly phenomena and, of course, the future.

APPENDIX

Table of City Numbers

City	*Country*	*City Number*
Addis Ababa	Ethiopia	2
Adelaide	South Australia	2
Aden	Southern Yemen	6
Agartala	India	7
Agra	India	7
Ahmedabad	India	9
Ajanta	India	4
Ajmer	India	4
Akola	India	5
Alexandria	Egypt	1
Aligarh	India	7
Allahabad	India	3
Ambala	India	3
Amravati	India	2
Amritsar	India	9
Amsterdam	Netherlands	1
Ankara	Turkey	3
Anuradhapura	Sri Lanka	6
Arcot	India	8
Asansol	India	5
Athens	Greece	5
Atlanta	USA	1
Aurangabad	India	8

City	*Country*	*City Number*
Ashburton	New Zealand	8
Asuncion	Paraguay	4
Arkonam	India	4
Auckland	New Zealand	7
Augsburgh	Germany	4
Badagara	Indonesia	6
Badin	Pakistan	4
Badulla	Sri Lanka	2
Balasore	India	6
Balsar	India	3
Baltimore	Ireland	2
Bangalore	India	3
Bangkok	Thailand	2
Bannu	Pakistan	1
Barcelona	Spain	2
Bareilly	India	9
Barletta	Italy	4
Barnet	UK	1
Beaumont	USA	7
Belgaum	India	6
Beijing	China	9
Beirut	Lebanon	2
Belfast	UK	8
Berlin	Germany	9
Bhuj	India	5
Bhusaval	India	9
Bijapur	India	3
Bijnor	India	9
Bikaner	India	9
Birmingham	USA	1
Boston	USA	1
Bradford	UK	3
Bridgeport	USA	2
Bristol	UK	4

City	*Country*	*City Number*
Bunbury	Australia	6
Burnio	Australia	3
Cairo	Egypt	5
Calcutta	India	7
Cambridge	New Zealand	7
Canberra	Australia	3
Canton	USA	7
Cape Town	South Africa	2
Chainpur	Nepal	4
Chandigarh	India	3
Chandrapur	India	1
Charleston	USA	1
Charlotte	USA	7
Chennai	India	6
Chicago	USA	5
Chikmagalur	India	4
Chitrakoot	India	9
Chittagong	Bangladesh	9
Chittoor	India	6
Christchurch	New Zealand	6
Cincinnati	USA	2
Clermont	Australia	6
Coimbatore	India	9
Collingwood	New Zealand	4
Cologne	Germany	5
Colombo	Sri Lanka	6
Colorado	USA	9
Columbia	USA	3
Connecticut	USA	1
Copenhagen	Denmark	2
Cuttack	India	5
Daman	India	6
Damascus	Syria	8
Dammam	Saudi Arabia	9

City	*Country*	*City Number*
Dannevirke	New Zealand	9
Dar-es-Salaam	Tanzania	9
Darjeeling	India	3
Darya Khan	Pakistan	4
Dehradun	India	5
Delhi	India	9
Detroit	USA	9
Devouport	Australia	3
Dhanbad	India	4
Digboi	India	9
Dinajpur	Bangladesh	1
Dispur	India	6
Diu	India	2
Doha	Qatar	8
Dubai	UAE	5
Durban	South Africa	2
Dusseldorf	Germany	9
Dunkrik	France	4
Durg	India	5
Edinburgh	UK	3
Elizabeth	USA	6
Eltham	New Zealand	1
Enfield	UK	4
Etawah	India	4
Eugene	USA	2
Ellichpur	India	9
Ernakulam	India	2
Etah	India	6
Faridabad	India	6
Florence	Italy	2
Faizabad	India	8
Ferozepur	India	5
Faridkot	India	2
Fatehgarh	India	7

City	*Country*	*City Number*
Freeport	Bahamas	5
Fremantle	Australia	1
Geneva	Italy	4
Georgia	USA	4
Gibraltar	Spain	1
Goa	India	2
Gorakhpur	India	9
Ghazni	Afghanistan	4
Gandhinagar	India	4
Garden City	USA	2
Gaue	Sri Lanka	6
Gaya	India	6
Gayndah	Australia	2
Ghaziabad	India	5
Guwahati	India	3
Hague	Netherlands	1
Hamirpur	India	2
Halifax	Canada	6
Hamilton	New Zealand	3
Hiroshima	Japan	2
Havana	Cuba	1
Haridwar	India	4
Helsinki	Finland	7
Helensville	New Zealand	8
Hisar	India	6
Hong Kong*	China	1
Hubli	India	8
Hyderabad	India	7
Hollywood	USA	7
Hoshiarpur	India	4
Houston	USA	1
Indore	India	6

* Hong Kong was acquired by Britain in 1898 by lease for 99 years. According to an agreement China recovered its sovereignty from 1 July, 1997.

City	*Country*	*City Number*
Imphal	India	5
Jaffna	Sri Lanka	6
Jagannath	India	6
Jaipur	India	1
Jaisalmer	India	3
Jalgaon	India	3
Jammu	India	7
Jerusalem	Palestine	3
Jeddah	Saudi Arabia	2
Jamnagar	India	9
Jodhpur	India	6
Jhansi	India	7
Jorhat	India	2
Johannesburg	South Africa	9
Jalandhar	India	5
Kabul	Afghanistan	5
Kandla	India	7
Kanpur	India	6
Kanyakumari	India	8
Kansas City	USA	6
Karachi	Pakistan	6
Kathmandu	Nepal	5
Karaikal	India	4
Khairpur	Pakistan	9
Kharagpur	India	3
Kimberley	South Africa	2
Kingston	New Zealand	1
Kodaikkanal	India	2
Kohima	India	2
Kolhapur	India	7
Kota	India	5
Kozhikode	India	4
Kuala Lumpur	Malaysia	7
Kuçhchaveli	Sri Lanka	2

City	*Country*	*City Number*
Kudat	Malaysia	8
Kupang	Indonesia	7
Kurnool	India	5
Kurukshetra	India	2
Lagos	Nigeria	8
Lahore	Pakistan	5
Lakewood	USA	8
Larkana	Pakistan	6
Las Vegas	India	7
Laura	Australia	4
Leeds	UK	2
Leh	India	4
Leicester	UK	4
Lexington	USA	2
Lismore	Australia	7
Liverpool	UK	6
London	UK	4
Long Beach	USA	7
Longreach	Australia	7
Los Angeles	USA	2
Louisiana	USA	1
Lucknow	India	5
Ludhiana	India	1
Madurai	India	1
Madrid	Spain	7
Madison	USA	7
Mahabaleshwar	India	3
Maho	Sri Lanka	8
Manchester	UK	1
Mangalore	India	1
Meerut	India	8
Mathura	India	5
Mecca	Saudi Arabia	7
Manila	Philippines	6

City	*Country*	*City Number*
Martinborough	New Zealand	6
Maryland	USA	3
Massachusetts	USA	9
Moradabad	India	8
Mirzapur	India	4
Miami	USA	2
Mussoorie	India	2
Mymensingh	Bangladesh	9
Nagasaki	Japan	8
Nagpur	India	7
Nagercoil	India	3
Nanjing	China	3
Napier	New Zealand	4
Naples	Italy	7
Narayanganj	Bangladesh	1
Nawabshaw	Pakistan	3
New Jersey	USA	6
New South Wales	Australia	5
New York	USA	1
Newport	UK	1
Nottingham	UK	3
Okara	Pakistan	4
Oklahoma City	USA	3
Osaka	Japan	5
Oxford	UK	6
Orlando	USA	2
Palakkad	India	5
Paeroa	New Zealand	6
Palermo	Italy	3
Palmerston	New Zealand	6
Panadura	Sri Lanka	1
Panipat	India	1
Pantnagar	India	3
Pathankot	India	1

City	*Country*	*City Number*
Patna	India	1
Pennsylvania	USA	7
Perth	Australia	6
Peterborough	UK	2
Pinjaur	India	3
Pisa	Italy	4
Pirojpur	Bangladesh	8
Plymouth	UK	2
Porbandar	India	5
Port Elizabeth	South Africa	6
Portsmouth	USA	5
Poltuvil	Sri Lanka	3
Pretoria	South Africa	3
Queensland	Australia	1
Quetta	Pakistan	3
Quorn	Australia	2
Queenstown	New Zealand	2
Raba	Indonesia	6
Rai Bareli	India	9
Raichur	India	2
Raigarh	India	6
Raipur	India	2
Rajahmundry	India	5
Rajkot	India	8
Rameswaram	India	2
Rampur	India	5
Ranikhet	India	7
Rapid City	USA	7
Ranchi	India	8
Raleigh	USA	2
Raglan	New Zealand	6
Rawalpindi	Pakistan	5
Richmond	USA	3
Riccarton	USA	1

City	Country	City Number
Rishikesh	India	9
Riyadh	Saudi Arabia	5
Rohtak	India	3
Rome	Italy	9
Rohanpur	Bangladesh	9
Rostock	Germany	1
Roxburgh	New Zealand	5
Rupnagar	India	1
Saharanpur	India	7
Sahiwal	Pakistan	2
Salt Lake City	USA	4
Sambalpur	India	3
San Diego	USA	2
Sandoway	Myanmar	1
Sandstone	Australia	1
Sandviken	Sweden	5
Sangrur	India	4
Santa Barbara	USA	7
Sarawak	Malaysia	7
Sargodha	Pakistan	8
Sarnath	India	3
Seattle	USA	7
Secunderabad	India	5
Semarang	Indonesia	6
Shahganj	India	6
Shahjahanpur	India	7
Seoul	South Korea	6
Shillong	India	3
Shimla	India	8
Sialkot	Pakistan	3
Shivpuri	India	5
Sivakasi	India	9
Somerset	Australia	6
South Dakota	USA	8

City	*Country*	*City Number*
Srinagar	India	8
Surat	India	7
Surab	Pakistan	5
Stratford	New Zealand	8
Sydney	Australia	1
Taiping	Malaysia	4
Takaka	New Zealand	2
Thimphu	Bhutan	6
Tenkasi	Indonesia	3
Thiruvananthapuram	India	4
Thanjavur	India	4
Tikamgarh	India	5
Tiruchirappalli	India	5
Tirupati	India	9
Tripoli	Libya	8
Tucson	USA	1
Tuensang	Indonesia	5
Tuticorin	India	6
Turbat	Pakistan	1
Turin	Italy	9
Udaipur	India	1
Ujjain	India	6
Unnao	India	6
Uran	India	5
Ulthai	Pakistan	8
Uttaradit	Thailand	9
Ustinor	Russia	5
Vadodara	India	8
Vaishali	India	3
Valletta	Malta	9
Vancouver	USA	5
Varanasi	India	2
Vatican City	Vatican City	3
Vellore	India	4

City	Country	City Number
Venice	Italy	6
Vermont	USA	6
Vienna	Austria	5
Vijaywada	India	4
Vrindavan	India	4
Waihi	New Zealand	5
Waipu	New Zealand	4
Walgett	Australia	8
Wana	Pakistan	4
Warangal	India	4
Warsaw	Poland	1
Washington D.C.	USA	2
Woodville	New Zealand	6
Wyndham	Australia	8
Xiamen	China	3
Xiangtan	China	7
Xining	China	2
Yamethm	Myanmar	8
Yanji	China	9
Yellowknife	Canada	1
Yokohama	Japan	1
Youngstown	USA	2
Zanthus	Australia	4
Zanjan	Iran	2
Ziarat	Pakistan	7
Zigong	China	8
Zurich	Switzerland	6

Index